11/03

CONSCIOUS STYLE HOME

CONSCIOUS STYLE HOME

ECO-FRIENDLY LIVING FOR THE 21ST CENTURY

DANNY SEO

ST. MARTIN'S PRESS
NEW YORK

For Ingrid,
who inspired it all

CONSCIOUS STYLE HOME: ECO-FRIENDLY LIVING FOR THE 21ST CENTURY. Copyright © 2001 by Danny Seo Media Ventures, Inc. All rights reserved. Printed in the United States of America. No part of this book may be used or reproduced in any manner whatsoever without written permission except in the case of brief quotations embodied in critical articles or reviews. For information, address St. Martin's Press, 175 Fifth Avenue, New York, N.Y. 10010.

www.stmartins.com

BOOK DESIGN BY MICHELLE McMILLIAN

Color photographs follow page 80.

Photographs on pages 9, 10, 31, 45, 61, 62, 75, 87, 153, and on color insert pages 2, 3, 4 (top and bottom left), 8 (top left and bottom), 11 (top and bottom left), 12, 13, copyright © Jennifer Levy. All other photographs copyright © Jonn Coolidge.

ISBN 0-312-27661-3

Printed on recycled paper

First Edition: September 2001

10 9 8 7 6 5 4 3 2 1

CONTENTS

ACKNOWLEDGMENTS

For years I've wanted to create a book about eco-friendly living that wasn't overwhelming or impractical. I wanted to provide simple, how-to information in a beautiful book with striking photography and user-friendly advice showing people how to create a comfortable, stylish living space without harming our planet. Because a book of this nature has never been done before, lots of people were involved, and they worked tirelessly to make *Conscious Style Home* a reality.

My editor, Julia Pastore, has been a dream to work with. In the busy world of publishing, where books are literally churned out overnight, her attention to detail, her sense of calm, and her undying support for the book have helped me immensely. I am fortunate to have this opportunity to work with such a professional and kind individual. And to everyone at St. Martin's Press—from editorial to marketing—you've done a phenomenal job. It's so refreshing (not to mention rare) for an author to work with such a talented team.

My literary agent, Joe Regal, has been with me ever since I started my career, just a few weeks out of high school. I don't really

Never sacrifice style for environmental reasons.

consider Joe an *agent*, but a friend who truly believes in my work; he's there to help guide me through a maze of chaos and confusion. Joe has been there through thick and thin. He makes my career as an author a true joy.

To everyone I work with in all my endeavors—Tom Carr, Angela Cheng, and Jodi Peikoff—thank you for your guidance, patience, and persistence. I wouldn't be who I am today without all of you.

Before I started writing this book, I sat down and pored through a hundred portfolios of different photographers so I could get the right look for the book. When I opened Jonn Coolidge's book, I knew from the start that he was the right person for the job. Talent like Jonn's is hard to come by. I'm honored to have him shoot my book. Many thanks to Warner Walcott and Michael DeJong for making the weeklong shoot go without a hitch. Also, thank you to Jennifer Levy for contributing some equally beautiful photos to the book.

To all the subcontractors, suppliers, experts, and public relations people I worked with (not to mention those to whom I pleaded and begged for product samples): thank you, thank you, thank you. I couldn't have done this book without all of you.

Finally, and most important: to my parents. Not for dealing with me for three months as I gutted their home, replanted the gardens, and painted the walls. Not for dealing with photographers (and their assistants) and movers (and their assistants) and contractors (and their assistants) and me (without an assistant) roaming around the house, and not for dealing with my late-night moments of inspiration when I would refinish a table at three o'clock in the morning, but for being great parents. All kids should be so lucky.

—Danny Seo

To me style is just the outside of content, and content the inside of style, like the outside and the inside of the human body— both go together, they can't be separated.

— Jean-Luc Godard

INTRODUCTION

I was born on Earth Day. Call it destiny, a major coincidence, or—as *the National Enquirer* boldly stated—an indication that I would one day "save more animals than Noah." Unless you're my mom, I certainly do not expect you to compare my environmental work to biblical legends. I do, however, think my birthday was the sole inspiration for my becoming an environmentalist.

In the early 1990s, I started my very own environmental group, Earth 2000, and it grew into the nation's largest youth conservation organization. That was the decade in which the whole world was gaining environmental consciousness. We looked in horror as the *Exxon Valdez* oozed crude oil into Prince William Sound. We shook our heads in disbelief at newscasts of the rain forests burning down. The hole in the ozone layer was scary. So we started to recycle. We brought our own shopping bags to the grocery store. And for a while, it seemed the world was going to work together once and for all to save the planet.

But how things have changed. In the late '90s, the environmental movement began to fade. We grew tired of seeing activists throw red paint on people wearing fur, or angry protesters chain themselves

LEFT: I enjoy finding hidden treasures in antique and vintage stores. BELOW: Don't forget the garden when you think of Conscious Style.

to trees. We thought, Isn't there another way to make a difference? Clearly, the eco-consciousness has never died, but the approach did. How could we apply our beliefs to day-to-day living? Maybe we don't have to spend the night in jail to make a difference. The small choices we make in our lives (what we eat and wear, how we furnish our homes), couldn't those decisions make an impact, too?

Fast-forward to today. One Saturday morning you decide to purchase new sheets. You're holding in one hand the organic cotton sheets that only come in shades of "natural," and in the other hand, a pretty pale blue 300-count sateen set. The right thing to do is buy the organic ones, but your evil side whispers in your ear that the sateen bedding is better looking, feels nicer, and is (surprise!) less expensive. So you leave the organic sheets behind. But still, you think as you hand the sales clerk your credit card, why couldn't the soft sateen sheets be organic? That would surely make your day.

That thought—my own and what I've heard from many others—is the inspiration for *Conscious Style,* a new philosophy that proves you can be really good to yourself—have a beautiful home, a stylish wardrobe, eat great food—and still care about the planet. When I bought a charcoal gray blanket on a whim one Saturday afternoon—the kind that was oh-so-soft and warm for those blustery winter nights—and noticed weeks later that it was made from recycled cashmere, I realized it was possible to be green *and* stylish. I didn't buy the blanket because it was eco-friendly. I bought it because it looked nice. I thought, Why do style and eco-consciousness have to be mutually exclusive? I don't think they do, and I've made it my mission in life to prove it.

What exactly is Conscious Style? First, Conscious Style ideas are made from recycled (and recyclable) materials. We all recycle, but recycling is worthless if we, the consumers, don't purchase items made from *recycled* materials. Second, the decorating solution must be well built and durable. A recycled glass tile that chips easily doesn't make sense when a subway tile will last for years to come. (Sometimes it's better to pick the stronger option over the recycled; a product that's made to last saves natural resources.) Third, Conscious

Style uses eco-friendly materials in a new and exciting way: concrete for kitchen countertops, wild latex from the rain forest to cover an ottoman, old bandannas sewn together to make a tablecloth. Finally—and this rule applies at all times—the idea must be aesthetically pleasing. Never sacrifice style for environmental reasons. While this may sound selfish, it's not—if you're not happy with a decision today, you're likely to change it tomorrow. You deserve a living space that is gentle on the planet and looks cool, too.

Another thing I've discovered by living the Conscious Style way is that I save money. Lots of us think eco-friendly products are expensive. But that simply isn't the case. Recycled paint costs significantly less than regular latex paint, bamboo shades are always inexpensive, and a set of handblown recycled glass tumblers costs about what you'd pay for a small pizza. Don't forget about the less obvious savings: My utility bills are lower, I'm entitled to tax breaks, and I'm healthier for creating a home free of harmful toxins.

For this book, I did something special: I renovated my parents' home. I didn't want to photograph turn-of-the-century castles or 3,000-square-foot SoHo lofts; I (and most of you) don't live that way. You'll notice that my parents' home is fairly typical: An exercise bike sits in the family room, misbehaving kitchen tiles are kept down with duct tape, piles of books have no place to go but on the floor. If I can transform this home, you can make yours into a stylish, comfortable living space, too.

On the following pages, you'll find the fruits of my effort, all designed with the same simple elegance and timeless styling that you've come to expect from any well-decorated home. I think you'll be pleasantly surprised to learn how easy Conscious Style living is. I trust this book will inspire you—whether it's to make a bed, paint a wall, redecorate a cluttered office, plant a garden, retile a bathroom, redo the kitchen . . . or to do your part to save the planet in the 21st century.

Oh, and those sheets . . . check out chapter 5, which is titled "Sanctuary." The time for aesthetically pleasing and luxurious organic cotton sheets has come.

CHAPTER ONE

LESS IS MORE

Sorting, Storing, and Maintaining

A clean desk is a sign of a cluttered desk drawer.

—ANONYMOUS

It's easy to let stuff take over your home. You don't live in a fantasy world where your house contains just a bed, a chair, a table, a pretty lamp, and a glass of water with a slice of lemon in it. Sure, those rooms in the photo shoots look pretty, but you've got books, clothes, and a collection of pottery, and you want to know what to do with them.

Fortunately, getting your home in order isn't difficult. I hope that after reading this chapter, you'll embrace my philosophy, which will help you get your home in order, keep you from scrambling to find that "thing that does the thing," and move you ahead toward gaining control of your stuff. Chaos . . . your days are numbered.

CLEANING UP

After I sold my first book to a publisher, I decided to celebrate by going on a shopping spree. I didn't buy a new car or a wardrobe of designer clothing. I bought furniture. And not just any old furniture, but the same high-caliber goods *House & Garden* editors want to

LEFT: A stainless-steel restaurant cart can be wheeled around the garage when needed; the metal locker bins are rust resistant and keep gardening tools organized. **BELOW:** Eco-friendly cleaners are easy to make with household products.

get their hands on. My shopping spree included a Frank Lloyd Wright reproduction side table, a vintage mission-style wood bed, a long steel table, and a green farmhouse-style chair with matching ottoman. The idea of spending a small fortune on a few pieces didn't seem wasteful to me; on the contrary, it seemed smart because I knew these items would be with me forever.

My apartment could have come right from the pages of a home-decorating magazine: exposed brick walls, hardwood floors, furniture placed just so, books stacked like a work of art. I liked spare living and didn't see why others couldn't live simply, too.

Soon I would eat my words. In a matter of months, my spare apartment became an eclectic mix of artifacts: autographed books from other authors, roadside finds, a metal sign warning WATCH YOUR BELONGINGS! WE ARE NOT RESPONSIBLE FOR STOLEN ITEMS! (The irony alone was enough to make me keep the sign.) In a matter of months, I was swimming in a sea of stuff. It was time to declutter.

I collected everything and sorted it based on the DRAGS system.

DUMP: Toss empty canisters, broken dishes, and anything that can't be recycled or is beyond repair. Don't feel bad about throwing away things that you can't find a use for; that's what the dump is for.

RECYCLE: It's amazing what can be recycled these days. A few years ago, only plastics coded #1 and #2, metal cans, and newspapers could be recycled; today, lots of recycling centers accept a myriad of plastics, metals, and paper products. Some communities will even recycle your old paint. Check with the local municipality about recycling options. The first few pages of the phone book usually have charts and guidelines about recycling. A few tips: Anything metal can usually be recycled—when I replaced the floor vents in my mom and dad's home, a local scrap metal dealer took them. Don't throw something into the recycling bin if you're not sure it can be recycled. It's actually eco-friendly not to recycle a bottle if you're unsure of its origins; otherwise, you might contaminate a load of recyclables, sending everything to the landfill.

Finally, don't throw away household hazardous wastes such as pesticides, paints, and herbicides. These contaminants can leak into the water supply if not properly disposed of. (In some communities it's illegal to throw away hazardous waste with the regular trash.) Contact your local government to find out how to dispose of it. And while you're at it, make a promise to yourself never to buy hazardous waste again; many Conscious Style solutions in this book will replace those toxic sprays.

ARTIFACT: Store anything that's irreplaceable, especially for sentimental reasons—photographs, mementos, artwork, important documents. Determine what items really are special to you—sometimes a *Dirty Dancing* ticket stub is just a ticket stub. Keep what you must and toss as much as you can.

GIVE: It's amazing how our garbage can actually help make a difference in the world. Old sneakers, for example, can be ground down and made into basketball courts. A bulky cell phone can be refurbished to help community watchdog groups; they're reprogrammed to dial 9-1-1 at the touch of a button. Here's the only tip about giving items to charity: Don't use donating as a way to indiscriminately get rid of your stuff. It'll get tossed if it's junk, disposal costs the charity time and money, and you're defeating the purpose of doing something good. Read the "Cash for Trash" section on giving to charity later in the chapter.

It's amazing what can be recycled—today, lots of recycling centers accept a myriad of plastics, metals, and paper products.

SELL: Why not make some money while you're at it? Used bookstores will pay cash for your never-read hardcover of *Ethan Frome*. Musical instruments, athletic gear, CDs and records, lightly used electronics, clothing, toys, baby gear, and furniture: There are lots of stores listed in the phone book that will pay cash on the spot for these things. And if you're feeling really generous, donate the proceeds to charity (and deduct it from your taxes).

Sometimes, good 'ol elbow grease can get the clean results you want.

Every year, when I apply DRAGS to my home, I discover that it's a wonderful way to relax. Honestly. Especially if you stop thinking of it as one more chore or a task to avoid by throwing some old sneakers into the trash. Done right, sorting through your belongings helps you come down off the weeklong mountain of stress, opens up lost memories in the course of uncovering photos and small trinkets from the past, and allows you to do a "clean sweep" of your surroundings, turning your cluttered home into a sanctuary.

GOING HOME

The very first thing I did when I began redesigning my parents' home was to evaluate how things were organized. Piles of worn-out sneakers, magazines, gardening tools, unfinished craft projects, and bulk-size cans of Campbell's Hearty Man soup were just a few of the items cluttering up the house. So I made a list of everything in the home that could go—to charity, the recycling center, or the landfill—and spent two hours hauling everything to the dump, to the curb for recycling, and to the Salvation Army. Already, the home looked better.

How do you know if something gets tossed? Start with the obvious: Recycle every magazine and catalog, remove your name from junk mail lists, remove every scrap and sheet of paper from the house—used or new. Instead, use a chalkboard to remind yourself to buy milk. Here are some other ideas:

OUT OF THE CLOSET. Push all your clothing to one end of the closet. Go ahead, jam it really good. Hang thirty hangers on the empty side. Now whenever you wear something, don't put it back on the jammed side, but hang it on an empty hanger. Do this every day. By the end of the month, see what you've worn and what just ends up gathering dust. Donate everything you haven't touched.

FOOD FIGHT. Go into your cupboard and refrigerator. Look at *everything*. What's expired or on the verge of going bad? Empty the contents of those containers down the garbage disposal (compost what you can) and recycle the empty jars, bottles, and boxes. Make a list of what you've tossed and especially of what you've thrown away in multiple quantities so you never buy it again.

FREE ISN'T FREE. When you check into a swanky hotel, are you one of those guests who waits for the maid to leave the cart unattended and raids it for those mini bottles of lotions, shampoo, and conditioner? Or do you go to a conference and find you can't leave without your free goodie bag? Or worse yet, have you tackled your grandmother to get the centerpiece at your sister's wedding?

Hauling all this free stuff home isn't really free—it clogs up your living space. After all, those little bottles just take up precious space in the medicine cabinet, those goodie bags just have catalogs and strange product samples, and that centerpiece will wilt in a few days. Instead, turn down those free things, sit back, and watch Aunt Frieda get tackled by Granny at the next wedding.

What you'll begin to notice as clutter is banished from your house is that treasured objects—a small oil painting by your mother, a vase, a lamp with an interesting patina—suddenly reappear once the clutter is gone.

Overaccessorized rooms are too busy, distracting, and unnerving to spend time in. Psychologically, clutter makes us feel weighed down or even overwhelmed. The message is unmistakable: Keep it simple.

USING WHAT YOU HAVE

I follow the mantra "It's not what you have, but how you use it." After you've eliminated a good portion of clutter using DRAGS, you're ready to refurnish your living spaces. Always start redecorating with what you have on hand.

When I began to refurnish the folks' house after the renovations, I designated a rarely used room, the guest bedroom, and brought in all the furniture and accessories from all the other rooms in the house. This room served as the central sorting area where I organized chairs, side tables, lamps, rugs, paintings, vases, and the like into their own separate areas.

By doing this, I began with a clean slate and could build new rooms the way I envisioned them. It's easier to redecorate a room when it isn't packed with furnishings and accessories. I moved a plant stand in the dining room, for example, into the bedroom to become a nightstand. That small kitchen dining table you were planning on replacing? Move it to the family room so you can have that writing desk you've always wanted.

Apply DRAGS to whatever is left in the central sorting room after you've finished decorating and get rid of it.

MAINTAINING

Once you've established order in your home, the next challenge is to maintain it. But the answer doesn't come in the form of plastic containers, boxes, and organizers (which only encourage you to acquire more things), but by evaluating the source of clutter: you.

Clutter happens for only two reasons. First, items are used and not properly stored. You need a pair of scissors, can't find the scissors, and buy a new pair. Soon, you end up with five pairs of scissors. The answer to this problem is fairly simple: Be more aware about putting items where they belong. Second, the front door is like a one-way street for things—bulk items from the grocery store, the spoils of a mad shopping spree, souvenirs from a vacation, piles of paperwork from the office—but nothing seems to be going *out*. The question isn't *how* this stuff accumulates, but *why* you accumulate it.

- Does having lots of goodies and things in the house make you feel more successful, comfortable, or loved?
- Are you afraid to throw something away because it's just too nice to toss or because you're worried that you might need it in the future?

- Do you still have empty cardboard boxes from major purchases you made several years ago?
- Do you save things because you think someone else might want them?

Take a good look around your house, and use these strategies to declutter:

GET DIGITAL. Buy a digital camera and banish that eco-evil disposable camera. Look at all those lovely pictures on the PC, and print the ones you really love.

While you're at it, replace your answering machine with voice mail; it'll get rid of that bulky machine. Get an Internet-based fax number; instead of getting faxes the old-fashioned way with paper printouts, you can access documents via your e-mail account. It works just like a regular fax, but you can store all those documents right on your computer. Visit www.efax.com and get an Internet fax account for free.

OUTLAW BIRTHDAY GIFTS. Have fun with friends and family instead of collecting gifts you'll most likely forget by next year. Send out an e-invite, ham it up with everyone at a corny karaoke bar, and cap the night with cake and champagne—or, have people give a donation to charity in your name. On my 12th birthday, I gave all my friends' gifts back to them and asked them to join me as members in an environmental group I was starting; everyone was happy to keep their original gifts, and their gift of time was something I truly appreciated.

CANCEL AUTOMATIC DELIVERIES. They were supposed to make your life easier and save you money, but they don't. Music clubs, fruits of the month, bath and beauty products from the TV . . . those cardboard boxes of stuff come to your house like clockwork.

Cancel all of them. And while you're at it, don't be tempted to sign up for a free trial of *anything*—magazines, coffees of the month, collector plates. Ignore them all.

SKIP THE MALL. Stop thinking of the mall as a recreation center; it's nothing more than a bunch of stores in an air-conditioned box. Spend your weekend doing more productive or relaxing things like going to a cabin by the lake, having a dinner party, or volunteering. When you do need to go shopping, go on a weekday when you don't have hours to spend in the stores. That way, you won't drop a small fortune on stuff you don't need.

CASH FOR TRASH

Ever hear the phrase "One man's trash is another man's treasure"? Your old stuff can be used to raise some serious cash for a good cause or, when you've got a selfish streak going, get you a few dollars closer to that dream vacation in the Amazon.

The three places where your used things can be donated, bought, and sold are called thrift, resale, and consignment stores. While they all deal with used merchandise, they conduct business quite differently.

A THRIFT STORE is run by a nonprofit organization to raise money to fund its charitable causes. Two national thrift-store chains are Salvation Army and Goodwill. When you donate items to these stores, you don't receive cash, but a receipt (for tax purposes) in the amount of the value of your deductible donation.

A savvy giver tip: Be wary of some thrift stores. Many thrift stores are run by for-profit companies that donate only a small percentage of total sales to charity—sometimes as little as 5 percent. When giving to a thrift store, ask what percentage of total sales benefits the charity, and be picky about who receives your generous contribution of merchandise.

A CONSIGNMENT STORE accepts merchandise on a commission basis, paying the owners of the merchandise a percentage when and if the items are sold, usually 50 percent of the selling price. For example, if they sell your shirt for $10, you'll receive $5 and they'll keep $5. If merchandise goes unsold, it will be returned to you or donated to charity.

RESALE STORES buy their merchandise outright from individual sellers. They range from pawnshops to high-end antique stores. Owners of these stores are more particular about what they accept, so don't take it personally if your merchandise isn't purchased.

The choice is yours: Donate your belongings to benefit charity, sell them to a resale store, or do both. If you decide to donate your lightly used belongings to a nonprofit organization, there are some rules to keep in mind.

Who knew trash could be recycled into such beautiful objects? These candlesticks are made from 100 percent aluminum.

FURNITURE

We all know that churches, charities, and humanitarian groups accept used furniture to give to people in need or for resale to benefit their organizations. There are specific guidelines to follow when donating used furnishings to charity:

- If you're thinking of donating a piece of furniture that you know is not reusable, don't donate it. Instead, discard it at a landfill. (Remove all metal parts beforehand and recycle them.)
- Waterbeds and upholstered furniture are difficult to donate. Charities aren't dumping grounds. If your furniture is not in reasonable shape, have it buried in a landfill.
- More valuable pieces of furniture should be sold to an antiques or used-furniture store. If you donate the proceeds to charity, get a receipt for your cash contribution.
- Used major appliances like refrigerators, ranges, and washers and dryers are not usually wanted by housing organizations like Habitat for Humanity. It's best to sell the appliance

Use old bandannas as covers and give pillows a face-lift.

over the Internet or with a classified ad and give the proceeds to charity. You can also place an ad in the local newspaper, usually for free, offering the appliance to any charitable organization. Should you get any takers, be sure to request a receipt for tax purposes.

CLOTHING

All of us have sweaters, pants, and jackets that we no longer wear. If you are (or wish to be) among the millions of people who donate clothing to charity every year, here are some simple steps to follow:

1. Wash your clothing. Fold all clothing (except shirts) and place in neat stacks in paper grocery bags.
2. Iron and starch any shirts; don't bag them, but suspend them on wire hangers. Save hangers you receive from the dry cleaner for this purpose.
3. Don't donate children's clothing with drawstrings around the neck. Because of safety regulations, thrift shops cannot sell any clothing that poses a choking hazard.
4. Don't give clothing with tears or holes in it; when in doubt, throw it away.
5. Give furs to an animal rights organization. Volunteers will use your furs to help educate the public about the cruelty of the fur industry.

CONSCIOUS STYLE GIVING

1. It's illegal to sell merchandise that has been recalled for safety reasons. Check with the Consumer Product Safety Commission (www.cpsc.gov or 800-638-2772) to ensure that any questionable items have met current safety standards before you donate or sell them.
2. Don't donate a bean bag chair. These chairs are filled with tiny pellets, which are a major choking and suffocating hazard for small children if they unzip the bag.

3. Use common sense. Items like paint, cleaning supplies, pillows, tires, and plumbing supplies are not wanted by charities. When people "donate" these items via a drop-off donation bin, it costs the charity money to have these items properly disposed of.

4. Clean all toys. According to Newborns in Need, a nonprofit organization that helps premature babies, "Most toys will go through the washer and dryer quite successfully . . . even baby dolls. Just make sure that toys and dolls that have fuzzy type fur or hair are air-dried or they will melt."

5. According to the Salvation Army, they frequently reject magazines, old encyclopedias, bathroom fixtures (toilets and the like), tires, swing sets, water heaters, windows, and doors. If it's trash to you, it's trash to them.

CHAPTER TWO

WALLS, WINDOWS, AND FLOORS

The window to the world can be covered by a newspaper.

—STANISLAW LEM

When was the last time your curtain, rug, or walls helped to make the world a better place? For most of us, the answer is never.

But the right material can do more than feel soft on your bare feet, block out light, or add color to your walls; it can help change the world. When I began choosing materials for my parents' home, I thought it would be a difficult process to locate eco-friendly options in a small community in Pennsylvania. To my surprise, I was able to source materials at national chain outlets and even local mom-and-pop stores. I even found materials on the Internet; all I had to do was type words like *hemp rug* or *bamboo blinds* into a Web search engine, and I'd be offered a myriad of beautiful options. As a bonus, most of the materials—from recycled paints to sisal rugs with canvas trim—were actually less expensive than their not-so-green siblings. With the money I saved, I could indulge in custom upholstery and purchase handmade tiles for the bathroom.

The foundation of any living space consists of three things: walls, windows, and floors. It all starts with choosing complementary colors

LEFT: A brass curtain rod, some clips, and a sheer tablecloth folded in half give privacy without blocking out the light. **BELOW:** Add unique yet simple accents like these blind pulls.

for the walls, ceiling, and trim: Color creates the mood (yellow for a cheery atmosphere, khaki for a sophisticated look). Window treatments should do more than add interest to the room; they must block out excessive light (or allow warm daylight in) and give privacy. Finally, and not least important, floors act like large canvases that accentuate the beauty of furniture. A Gustav Stickley chair will never look good on powder blue carpet. Like the perfect frame for a painting, your walls, windows, and floors set off whatever is in the room—giving neutrals depth and dimension, and colors a unifying ground. Choosing materials for these three components is the most important decision you'll make when creating a Conscious Style home.

IF THESE WALLS COULD TALK

It's often been said that if you can do only one thing to change a room, paint the walls. I couldn't agree more. But use a traditional latex paint, and you've got to open windows for ventilation, wear rubber gloves and a mask, and follow complex laws to safely dispose of any leftover paint. Is painting a wall a pretty mossy green, well, "green"?

The fact is that most of us are using the wrong paints. If you were like me a few years ago, you might've thought, "There are different types of paint?" The good news is that buying eco-friendly paint doesn't have to be complicated or expensive. All you have to do is look for four types of paint—recycled, industrial, VOC-free, and biodegradable.

RECYCLED PAINTS: They're smooth to work with and available in a variety of beautiful colors like Whipped White, Tawny Beige, and Juniper.

What is recycled paint? First, a fact: The average household disposes of one to three gallons of paint a year. Rather than dispose of leftover paint in a landfill, which is costly and harmful to the environment, companies like Amazon Environmental and e-Coat accept and reprocess leftover paints to create high-quality, economical re-cycled paint. And because there seems to be a limitless supply of old latex paint, the finished product retails for only pennies to the dollar of what traditional paint costs. *It costs less than regular paint with no difference in quality.*

INDUSTRIAL STRENGTH: For high-traffic areas—like the backyard deck—I didn't use recycled paint. Not because it is inferior in quality, but because latex paint, which is the only recycled kind available, is the wrong choice for the job. Instead, I used a tough-as-nails indus-trial paint, the same kind used in factories. Paint it once, the manu-facturer promised, and it'll last a lifetime.

I used a 100 percent acrylic latex paint because of its high-gloss finish, easy adhesion to previously treated wood, and its good resist-ance to scuffing, fading, cracking, peeling, and blistering. Because floor enamel can be harmful to the environment if improperly used (the ground surrounding the deck must be pro-tected so that spills don't enter the soil) or dis-posed of, I hired a local contractor to paint the deck. The contractor assured me that all environmental considera-tions would be handled, and by hiring someone, I saved a lot of time.

> I chose simple window treatments, purchasing bamboo and natural canvas blinds that pull open to let warm daylight pour into the house.

Another choice is industrial enamel paint. Industrial enamel paints are formulated to inhibit rust when applied over properly prepared surfaces such as cast-iron or steel fences, gates, railings, doors, hardware, and roofs. Floor deck enamels are harder than house paint, and they resist abrasion from foot traffic. Synthetic resins such as urethane, polyurethane, or epoxy are added to in-crease hardness and durability. Industrial enamel paint can be tinted up to 1,200 different custom colors and can protect outdoor fixtures from the elements.

It's true that acrylic latex and industrial enamels aren't made from eco-friendly ingredients, but they are an extremely durable option. Many of these paints come with a lifetime guarantee. Because you'll use these paints sparingly for areas that are subject to harsh conditions or high traffic, like the deck, kitchen floor, or garage, they'll prevent future repairs and protect your investment for years to come.

VOC-FREE: Most air toxins are organic chemicals, made of carbon, hydrogen, and other atoms called Volatile Organic Compounds (VOCs). In addition to being harmful to our health, VOCs contribute to urban smog and to the earth's greenhouse effect, one of the biggest causes of global warming. VOCs are created in the production of plastics, which are found in gasoline and in paint. Virtually chemical and odor-free, VOC-free paints are a good choice for those who are chemically sensitive.

VOC-free paints are available in a preparation that is nonpolluting and friendly to the environment. They work just like regular paint, can be cleaned up with water, and dry quickly. I painted the family room with Sherwin-William's HealthSpec, a low-VOC paint in Primitive Green. It costs a little bit more than traditional paint, but because I am sensitive to chemicals, the few extra dollars were worth it.

BIODEGRADABLE: In the last decade, numerous and complex procedures for the disposal of paint and other household hazardous waste have made a weekend paint job more complicated than calling the IRS with a "simple" tax question. But homeowners who ignore the rules are liable for penalties. Thankfully, one entrepreneur has come up with a solution: 100 percent biodegradable paint.

In 1982, Rudolph Reitz decided to create an environmentally safe, natural paint that works well, looks good, and is a pleasure to use. His BioShield Paints are made from simple ingredients that are easy to pronounce: citrus peel oils and solvents, essential oils, seed oils, tree resins, inert mineral fillers, tree and bee waxes, lead-free dryers, and earth pigments. They work just like regular paint. The best part is the options: You can custom tint the paints or choose from a palette of beautiful colors like Aurora Yellow, Terra Fuego, or Terra Verde Green.

Milk paint is another good choice. Early American colonists and Shakers painted their furniture and interiors with milk paint using a formula that dates back to ancient Egypt. Milk paint consists of milk protein, clay, earth pigments, and lime.

While milk paint may not saturate walls as well as latex paint, its distinctive finish, which is flat and coarse, lends a nostalgic look to walls and furniture. It's best to stick with muted colors (shades of red, blue, yellow, and orange) based on historical hues and made from earth pigments like ocher, umber, and iron oxide. After painting the wall, you can create a beautiful translucent finish by rubbing an all-natural wax on the surface. Not only does wax add beauty and luster, but it will also help repel dirt and dust from the finish.

CONSCIOUS STYLE SOLUTION: AGING WALLPAPER

In one of my favorite restaurants in New York City, the wallpaper appears aged from several decades of patrons smoking cigars and cigarettes. But Pastis is a new restaurant, and the look wasn't achieved with the help of tobacco but with a simple tea-staining method. By tinting the walls with a brown glaze and wiping away the excess with a soft cloth, the gleaming new wallpaper took on a rich, warm patina.

Tea-staining wallpaper is a great way to change the look of a room, add character, and salvage wallpaper that would otherwise need to be scraped, trashed, and replaced. To "age" a wall, first you must determine if the existing wallpaper is a good candidate. Simple floral prints and vintage patterns work well; the end results look as if the walls have endured fifty years of sun and smoke. Modern designs, on the other hand, do not work; staining them only distorts the wallpaper and makes it look dirty.

If your wallpaper passes muster, prepare the room as you would for a paint job. Use a canvas drop cloth to protect the floors, and tape off any wood molding or trim. Gather the tools you'll need for the project: paint tray, roller, and a pile of lint-free cloth rags.

Staining a wall is simple: Roll on the glaze (a lighter glaze for "sun fade" or a darker one for "smoke"), and wipe off the excess with the rags to soften the tinting. (See resource guide for manufacturers.) Allow the surface to dry thoroughly before reapplying the glaze, if needed. In just a few minutes, you've time-warped your walls and added instant patina and charm.

WINDOWS TO THE WORLD

Windows are an ancient invention, contrived when the first enclosed house was constructed. Windows allowed mankind to live indoors without being deprived of light and air from outdoors. According to early Egyptian wall paintings, windows were large openings in house walls covered with matting to block out the light. In the baths of ancient Rome, windows were covered to retain the heat.

Today, windows are more energy-efficient and easier to maintain than in the past. They are also available in a seemingly limitless number of shapes and designs. But even as windows become

21st-century wonders, some of us have window treatments reminiscent of the ancient Egyptians: An oversize plastic blind is haphazardly hung or, as in my friend's home, a large terry towel is staple-gunned to a window.

Chances are you own a collection of curtains, blinds, and shades, all rolled up or folded in cardboard boxes in the closet. And it's no wonder that you keep them in a box and not on the windows—most of them didn't fit, didn't do their job, or simply looked awful in the room.

At my parents' home, yards of flowery fabric had been hung as window treatments. Poles and plastic-coated wire (all from an infomercial on TV that hyped "an easy way to dress up the window") twisted, folded, and fanned the fabric into an unrecognizable mess. The problem was twofold: The curtains didn't effectively block out light, and the sheer size overpowered the room. To solve this problem, I chose simple window treatments, purchasing bamboo and natural canvas blinds that pull open to let warm daylight pour into the house.

It is tempting to take yards of luxurious fabric and create billowy, fanciful curtains that could easily be mistaken for an ostentatious ball gown. (Remember Carol Burnett wearing a curtain in a spoof of *Gone With the Wind*?) Window treatments, however, should never be the focus of a room; they should serve their utilitarian purpose and feature basic, monochromatic materials that aren't busy or bold. Choose natural materials—like wood, canvas, hemp, and bamboo—for your windows. What's great about using natural materials is that they are easy to work with, inexpensive, and they really do serve their purpose. You can block out light or allow it in, and the blinds look great pulled up or down. The best part is that there's no need to hire a decorator to "pouf" or twist fabric; with a cordless drill, a screwdriver, and some hooks, you can do it yourself in minutes. And always keep in mind the easiest window treatment: none at all. A bare window to the world frames the outside—green trees, a blue sky dotted with fluffy clouds, a bird sitting on the windowsill—like a piece of ever-changing artwork.

Bamboo is one of the most eco-friendly materials you can purchase. I ordered these custom-made blinds on the Internet, and they arrived at my door in just a few weeks.

FLOORED

You probably haven't thought about your floors in a long time. ("Let's see . . . buy bread, pick up kids, think about floors. . . .") When my parents built their home in 1987, my mother picked vinyl floors for the kitchen, hardwood for the living and dining rooms, and simple beige wall-to-wall carpeting for the rest of the house.

Back then, which is to say not that long ago, flooring options were limited to synthetic carpet, hardwood floors, tile, and linoleum; the greatest innovation in flooring at the time was stain-resistant carpeting. Consumers demanded easy-care floors, and that's what manufacturers provided. My mother didn't consider her floors blank canvases, and she certainly didn't consider the environmental impact of her choices; she simply picked what seemed sensible.

Only relatively recently has there been growing concern about flooring and how it affects the environment and our health. Conventional wall-to-wall carpet has been found to contribute to poor air quality in homes, and concern for our forests has prompted many people to forfeit the use of hardwood floors altogether. Companies now offer homeowners options that are good Conscious Style choices. Today, hand-poured recycled glass tiles, all-natural wall-to-wall sisal and hemp carpeting, and wood floors made from sustainably harvested wood and unconventional materials like bamboo and reclaimed timber are easy to find and available in a wide assortment of colors and textures.

With all these choices, which one do you pick for your home? First, assess the room you are renovating—you will need to take into consideration its size and use. While a seagrass rug may look beautiful in the bathroom, it's not a wise choice: Once seagrass gets wet, it begins to decompose. Hemp, which can withstand moisture, is a good alternative. Do you want easy-care floors for the kitchen? If so, consider old-fashioned linoleum (not the vinyl kind, but those made from natural resins popular in the 1940s), poured concrete, or large terra-cotta tiles, which reflect heat and stay cool in the summer. Is the family room used frequently? Choose a hardwood floor with a high Janka hardness (a measurement of the force needed to embed a .444-inch steel ball into half the diameter of a piece of wood; the higher the number, the harder the wood) so dents and scratches will be kept to a minimum. Also consider a pre-finished hardwood to save you time and trouble. Most certified hardwood floors are finished with nontoxic sealers that accentuate the beauty of the wood and protect it from the elements.

Once you've discovered the numerous choices available for your floors, you may never look at them the same way again.

WOOD YOU?

Responsible logging may sound like an oxymoron, but a group of concerned businessmen is working hard to change that. The Forest Stewardship Council, an independent organization that monitors sustainable logging practices, has created the first forest product certification program to identify wood products that meet stringent environmental standards.

Why create a certification process? When looking at wood floors, you may come across labels that describe a manufacturer's commitment to the environment. These claims, "We replant twice as many trees as we harvest" and even "certified," mean nothing without a third-party monitoring system in place.

The Forest Stewardship Council guarantees that the certified wood floors consumers are installing in their homes are from trees that were harvested in the most ecologically sensitive way possible. Old-growth forests and environmentally sensitive areas are left intact. Instead, managed forests with selective logging—real methods that truly protect the biodiversity of a forest—are supported. By tracking wood from the forest to final product, certifiers enable consumers to support responsible forestry and provide forest owners with economic incentives to maintain forest-management techniques.

FSC-certified wood products can be found in home improvement stores and through a comprehensive directory available at the council's Web site, www.fscus.org. By spending a few extra minutes searching for the certification symbol, you'll tread lightly on the planet every time you walk across your new hardwood floors.

A little bit of contrast goes a long way. The compressed reeds of the bamboo plant give the floor a strong vertical rhythm. The footstool is made from dried water hyacinth, an invasive plant collected by local artisans in Africa and woven into fine furniture.

BAMBOO. Bamboo floors aren't made from trees, but from giant, fast-growing grasses that have woody stems. Native to tropical and subtropical and temperate regions, bamboo grows quickly—as much as one foot *per day*. To transform bamboo into beautiful flooring, it is cut and milled into long thin strips, laminated together into a single-ply veneer, and then compressed under heat and pressure to create a multilayer plank.

I installed bamboo floors in my parents' bedroom because of its strength (its Janka hardness is comparable to that of maple) and unique appearance; the long, straight vertical lines added a visual rhythm to the room and gave the floor a sense of uniformity that I found calming.

TANOAK. A member of the beech family, tanoak is native to coastal areas of southern Oregon and northern California. Its wood is naturally a reddish light-brown color and is often used for handles on gardening tools and in furniture. It's also a great mulch; when using unfinished tanoak floors, the scrap wood can be fed through a wood chipper and spread in the garden.

HEART PINE. Also known as the longleaf pine, heart pine is a slow-growing tree from the northwest section of the United States. Because of its slow growth, the tight graining is the densest of all pines. The wood has a natural reddish tinge throughout, and its high Janka hardness makes it an excellent choice for flooring in high-traffic areas.

HARD MAPLE. Used for lumber, wall paneling, flooring, furniture, handles, interior finish, cabinets, and novelties, hard maple is also known as sugar maple and black maple. Grown in the Mississippi Valley and in the eastern United States, the wood is a cream to slight reddish brown color, strong, stiff, and extremely resistant to shock. Usually straight grained, hard maple can also have curly or wavy grain.

ASH. The next time you're rowing a boat, you're most likely holding ash wood in your hands. Ash wood is naturally light colored or

nearly all white and grown in the eastern part of the United States. Old-growth ash trees are rare because of years of logging and clear-cutting. Second-generation trees are highly sought after, however, because of their strong, stiff qualities and high resistance to shock. (Most baseball bats are made from ash.)

HARDWOOD MADRONE. It was first marketed in the early 1900s as California black cherry. Its color compares closely to Eastern cherry and ranges from light salmon to deep burgundy. Madrone's high density gives it a great advantage over cherry: It makes sense for use as a kitchen cabinet if you want the look of cherry, but with added strength and durability.

MACHICHE. When Sting and the Martin Guitar Company teamed up to make a limited edition Sting Signature guitar, the die-hard environmentalist and Grammy-award-winning singer wanted to use exotic, certified wood. Machiche is a visually attractive wood whose color compares to that of rosewood and mahogany.

Chosen as flooring for Banana Republic stores in California because of its high Janka hardness, machiche is also very resistant to fungi attack and is therefore a good choice for humid areas. The dark reddish brown hardwood polishes to a lustrous finish and is a good choice for flooring, furniture, and countertops.

I'VE GOT YOU COVERED

Did you know that the first rugs were made by twisting threads of grass and hair into a crude mat?

Such prehistoric rawness reminds me of my favorite all-natural rugs. Even as our floors over the years may have been covered with green shag carpet, rugs made of natural sisal, coir, or jute always make a comeback because of their rugged good looks and strong texture.

It's no wonder: Natural rugs have great warmth and appeal. The earth tone coordinates well with almost any decor, and the durability and ease of care can't be beat. Natural rugs are rough enough to withstand a daily scratching from any ferocious feline and soft enough to feel warm and fuzzy on our bare feet. Best of all, many of them are affordable and easy to find.

SISAL. Sisal originates from a large leafy plant native to Central America and is grown on farms all over the world. Large rosettes are harvested from the plant and crushed between rollers; the pulp is scraped away, dried, and woven to create long strands of fiber. Coarse in texture, sisal is strong, durable, easy to stretch, and resistant to natural elements. In the family room, I replaced the old carpet with wall-to-wall sisal. It was strong enough that people could walk on it with their shoes on, luxurious in texture to add beauty to the room, and less expensive than standard wall-to-wall nylon carpet.

HEMP. More commonly known for producing the narcotic drug marijuana from its leaves and blossoms, hemp is produced from the plant *Cannabis sativa*. Industrial hemp is grown without the use of pesticides, insecticides, or herbicides. The woody plant grows like, well, a weed—up to nine or ten feet tall. A strong and durable fiber, hemp is naturally yellowish, greenish, or dark brown; in Italy, hemp is processed to create a finer, whitish fabric that is similar in texture to fine linen. Hemp rugs are considerably more expensive than other natural rugs, but that's the price you pay for rugs that come with a lifetime guarantee.

JUTE. Historically, jute fiber was imported from the Bengal area of India and primarily used for cordage. Today, jute is used for a variety of products, including burlap bags for the shipment of grains and feed, backing for fine rugs, rope, and mats and rugs. A good jute rug should be framed with a border of canvas; the canvas will prevent the edges of the rug from deteriorating.

COIR. Collected from the outer shell fiber of the coconut, the coarse, reddish brown fiber is lightweight, strong, and elastic. Because it has a natural tendency to curl at the edges, coir rugs are usually reversible, so they can be flipped monthly to keep the rugs flat. Coir rugs are an ideal choice for dry, dusty areas since dirt will not lie on top of the rug but will instead fall through onto the floor underneath. I placed a coir rug on the outdoor deck in the protected area; to clean, all I have to do is lift up the rug, vacuum or sweep the debris away, and set the rug back into place.

SEAGRASS. Grown throughout China, seagrass is woven into rugs that resemble straw rugs, but have a silkier, smoother texture than sisal, jute, or coir. Don't use seagrass in humid areas—like the bathroom or outdoors—since water can damage this material.

TATAMI. On my first book tour in South Korea, I was intrigued by a mat I found in my hotel room made entirely from woven grass. Called *tatami,* these mats originated in Japan over two thousand years ago and are common in most Asian households. The all-natural rugs serve a number of purposes: They absorb humidity, ventilate heat, and are believed to freshen the air. When used to cover a hard floor surface—like hardwood or concrete—the mat gently massages the feet, helping to stimulate blood circulation.

I use tatami mats outdoors, placing them on the grass or on the beach. The light mats can be rolled up and transported.

TILE AND CONCRETE

If you want flooring that is more rugged than wood or natural rugs, investigate concrete and tile floors.

CONCRETE. The earliest version of concrete consisted mostly of clay and was used among the ancient Assyrians and Babylonians. The formula didn't change until 1824 when an English inventor, Joseph Aspdin, burned and ground together a mixture of limestone and clay to form what resembles modern concrete. This recipe, called portland cement, has remained pretty much unchanged to this day.

When one thinks of concrete, interior floors and countertops don't usually come to mind; the garage floor and sidewalk are probably the only concrete around the house. And you probably wouldn't describe it as pretty, either.

When you take any plain material and use it in an unconventional way, its rawness shines. Having wall-to-wall concrete floors—polished smooth and then treated with acid to give a burnished look—frames your furniture and belongings to look like pieces of art. I compare it to serving meals on simple white plates—the food just looks great, doesn't it?

TERRA COTTA. Literally translated as "baked earth," terra cotta became widely used in the fifth century when the Della Robbia family discovered a way to glaze it as an accent material. Soon the use of terra cotta in sculpture and home building spread from Italy throughout Europe. Today, terra cotta remains pretty much the same utilitarian, versatile, durable, and inexpensive material—perfect for almost any room in the house.

Terra cotta begins as a porous clay that, when fired, assumes a color ranging from dull ochre to red; when glazed, the terra cotta becomes stronger and takes on a shiny, finished appearance.

In warmer areas of the world, terra cotta is used widely for flooring because of its ability to repel heat and keep flooring cool. Its natural color blends in well with almost any decor, and if a tile should chip or break, replacing the cracked tile is a job the novice craftsman can do.

CONSCIOUS STYLE PROFILE: ECOTIMBER

In a converted 25,000-square-foot warehouse in Berkeley, California, some planks of wood are about to meet their new owner. The wood has taken a long journey to get there. The flooring was cut by lumberjacks in the late 19th century from old-growth redwood trees. After a 100-year stint as support beams and floors in an industrial factory in northern California, these planks and wooden poles were carefully salvaged with the same care that the rarest of museum artifacts would receive. What normally would be buried in the landfill has been given a second chance at life. From there, the reclaimed lumber—with a warm patina that can only come from decades of aging by the elements—will become beautiful flooring in someone's kitchen and perhaps architectural details in a spare New York City loft.

As an activist for groups like Greenpeace and the Rainforest Action Network, San Francisco native Jason Grant saw a burgeoning trend: lumber made from sustainable woods and quality old-growth reclaimed timber. There was growing concern about deforestation in the late 1980s, so Grant recognized an untapped market of homeowners and design professionals wanting to use ecologically sound woods. So he started EcoTimber, an ecological supplier of exotic and domestic woods. "I saw an opportunity to have financial security and still make a difference," Grant said.

"A brand is a promise," is how Grant likes to describe his business. Nothing about this company strays from Jason's commitment to provide sustainably harvested timber for craftspeople, design professionals, and store builders. From the start, Jason and his business partners, Aaron Maizlish and Eugene Dickey, made a decision to sell only the most ecologically sound woods available, personally monitoring their sources to ensure they meet EcoTimber's high ecological and social standards. The company's domestic and overseas suppliers must

1. commit themselves to long-term forest management in which timber growth equals or exceeds harvesting rates in both quality and quantity;

(continued)

2. harvest and extract timber using methods that preserve the fundamental ecological integrity of the forest, maintain wildlife habitat, and minimize damage to soil and watersheds;

3. recognize and promote the land-use rights and land ownership of local communities;

4. fairly compensate working participants.

EcoTimber's philosophy has proved successful. The company provides flooring for individuals and corporations who want beautiful hardwood floors in their homes and businesses but don't want to see our majestic rain forests and old-growth forests clear-cut. "We really are on the cutting edge of a new industry," Grant said. Even talk show host Jay Leno is a fan. On the *Tonight Show* set, the desk and drink tables are made from EcoTimber exotic woods. Customers initially purchase EcoTimber products because of social responsibility; they keep coming back for the quality.

With revenues now approaching $4 million annually, Grant is finding ways to "give back" by bettering the lives of young people. As part of its efforts to reclaim timber from warehouses, bridges, and buildings, EcoTimber teamed up with the Youth Employment Partnership (YEP), a nonprofit agency that provides job training to economically disadvantaged youth in Oakland, California. YEP participants deconstruct old warehouses that contain thousands of board feet of old-growth lumber. Not only are young people picking up valuable environmental lessons, they learn employment skills, earn money, and are empowered to understand that success is within their reach. www.ecotimber.com.

RECYCLED. For the bathroom, I decided to keep the color scheme simple. The walls were painted white, the ceiling a light blue high-gloss paint, and the tile, my mother decided, should be "a very simple, clean color." While white subway tile might seem like the best solution, the problem was that it looked too plain. And because the room was relatively small, measuring only five feet by eight feet, there was no reason to be too concerned about cost. I splurged and bought handmade recycled glass tiles.

A small company in Alaska named Sandhill Industries manufactures beautiful tile made entirely from recycled glass. Old soda bottles, spaghetti jars, and other glass recyclables are separated by color, melted down, and poured into molds. While one might think glass floor tiles would crack and chip easily, they're actually stronger than ceramic tile. Ceramic is baked clay coated with glass for strength; a glass tile is 100 percent glass, which is actually twice as strong as ceramic.

The translucent tile, in a wide variety of colors ranging from fully saturated hues to clear with whispers of color, are luxurious in weight, depth, and texture.

INDUSTRIAL. I often find myself staring at the wall or floor inside a New York City subway terminal, admiring the simple beauty of industrial tile. Installed for its ability to withstand the abuse of millions of commuters, industrial tile is finding its way into homes.

Inexpensive, strong, and free of ornamentation, industrial tile works well in the home.

In areas of the home like the kitchen and bathroom, industrial tiles make sense. For the backsplash in the kitchen, which is often splattered with hot oil and banged with copper pots, white subway tile is durable, easy to clean, and simple enough in appearance. In a larger bathroom, using smaller tiles—one- or two-inch tiles are good choices—allows you to invest more money in installation to lay the intricate tile in an unusual pattern. White tile won't look busy in a creative design the way color or patterned tile would.

DISPOSAL OF FLOORING

For most of us, recycling aluminum cans, newspapers, and empty spaghetti sauce jars is not a big deal. But when was the last time you hauled a pile of old, worn carpet to the recycling center? The good news is that carpet is one home product you can do something about.

The Environmental Protection Agency estimates that a whopping 2 percent of total waste in landfills is from carpet alone. Virtually all the carpet in the world (excluding natural rugs like sisal, hemp, and jute) is made from nylon. When buried in a landfill, as most old carpet is today, it does not decompose. What could that carpet possibly be recycled into? Plenty. When shredded and recomposed into a raw material known as Nylon 6, it can be made into products such as residential and commercial carpet, engineering plastics, automotive parts, sporting goods, films, and packaging.

There are plenty of recycling facilities willing to take your old carpeting. Start by contacting Evergreen Nylon Recycling in Augusta, Georgia. Already recycling 200 million pounds of post-consumer carpet a year (and saving 700,000 barrels of oil, too—enough to heat 100,000 homes), Evergreen collects used carpet from all over the United States. The service isn't free, but the fee is competitive with landfill or disposal costs. Call (877) N6-CYCLE to learn more.

Also contact your local sanitation department. They can provide a wealth of information on what to do with unusual refuse items.

CHAPTER THREE

COOKING AND ENTERTAINING

At my age the bones are water in the morning until food is given them.

—PEARL BUCK

If you're like me, you've discovered the joys of organic produce. Not only is organic produce good for the environment, but the apples are crisp and tart, the tomatoes are firm and ripe, and the peaches taste the way Mother Nature meant them to be: sweet and oh-so-juicy.

My kitchen reflects the way I buy my groceries. The Conscious Style kitchen is a place where you can get those post-holiday dishes sparkling clean, whip up a wild mushroom risotto just like your favorite restaurant does, and make stove S'Mores on a cold winter night. It's a place not only built with eco-friendly materials and energy-efficient appliances, but it marries functionality with great looks, too.

You might also be surprised to learn that better, smarter design over the years from mainstream kitchen supply manufacturers has created a wealth of affordable and easy-to-find Conscious Style kitchen solutions out there. Richly colored wood cabinets, for example, don't have to come from endangered rain forests or old -growth

LEFT: Here, Melissa Hicks, my best friend since childhood, joins me for a quick bite during the photo shoot. BELOW: Recycled glassware from GreenGlass looks pretty on this serving piece.

trees. Instead, beautiful cabinets are now made from certified "green" wood or super-durable wood laminate that, unlike the '70s version, is free of toxic glues and chemicals.

A CLEAN KITCHEN

Renovating my parents' kitchen was a surprise. I expected the process to be difficult, imagining nightmarish scenarios of trying to locate energy-efficient appliances and certified green cabinetry in this small town.

But I was astonished: Wood veneer cabinets, made with sustainably harvested wood and nontoxic glues, recycled glass tiles, eco-friendly tableware, and energy-efficient appliances were available locally and on the Internet. With a few phone calls, e-mails, a visit from UPS, a meeting with a local subcontractor, and a few days of construction, the kitchen was completed.

CABINETS. Some kitchen cabinets light up the room. Others are a real drag. Good kitchen cabinets don't have to be expensive or custom-made. Ever since giving the kitchen a face-lift became the most popular home renovation, the process seems to be getting less complicated. At some stores, like IKEA, you can walk in unannounced, design a kitchen in a few minutes, and walk out with a blueprint.

Now that one step has become painless, let's talk about the environment. Cabinets made from noncertified rain-forest wood are obviously bad for the environment. But what about cabinets that can make you sick? Puce laminate may be gross to look at, but the materials and glues used to put those cabinets together can actually affect your physical health.

Formaldehyde is the enemy here. The same nauseating smell from biology class is found in most cabinets. The glue used to put wood cabinets together contains a high level of formaldehyde, which over time evaporates into the atmosphere: your home. There are alternatives. One company, Becker Zeyko of Germany, manufactures wood cabinets that are made from sustainably harvested wood and are 100 percent free of formaldehyde and polyvinyl chloride (PVC), which is good since these chemicals form a poisonous gas if there's a fire in the home. With over two hundred different cabinet styles to choose from, Becker Zeyko isn't small potatoes in the kitchen cabinet market. More and more, formaldehyde-free cabinets are easier to find.

If wood isn't your style, metal is a good option. There's absolutely no formaldehyde in metal cabinets, and your kitchen will have an efficient and attractively modern look. The option has grown in popularity over the years, and now major kitchen renovation centers often carry several all-metal cabinet designs.

COUNTERTOPS. The best countertops are expensive. And they're worth every penny. If you're going to splurge, spend it on the countertops. But a good countertop should do more than look pretty; it should help you make cooking more enjoyable. Stainless steel, for example, is easy to keep clean while real wood can take a real beating.

Don't let that lower price tag tell you that laminate countertops look just like wood or stone. They will chip, burn, and discolor.

Okay, now for the Conscious Style part: Not all stone and wood countertops are alike. The price, color, and availability of any of Mother Nature's creations will differ in a dizzying number of options, but the environmental impact, fortunately, is really simple to understand.

MARBLE. Some materials, no matter how gorgeous they are, belong just where we find them. Marble countertops are not kind to the environment. Marble is found deep in the earth, and to quarry it out, channeling machines with chisel-edged steel bars cut deep into the ground. After leaving scars and large gaping holes in the earth, at least half the marble extracted is waste.

If you must have marble for its good surface for rolling dough or pastry making, fine, but there's no need to cover the *whole kitchen* with it. Instead, get a large scrap piece from the kitchen supply store or hardware store; chip the sides to give it a natural form and sit it on top of another countertop. A square three-foot piece should do for all your baking needs.

GRANITE. If you want the look of marble but not the guilt, choose granite. Granite is an igneous rock cooled within the earth where it forms into a molten state. It is made up mainly of quartz (which makes it durable) along with some feldspars and mica (which gives it flecks of color and depth). Unlike marble, granite is found near the surface and can be obtained without the use of strip mining. This is a material that can be quarried with the least environmental impact.

And here's a Conscious Style tip: Ask local kitchen renovation centers if they will sell you the leftover granite from previous kitchen renovation jobs. These slabs of granite, which aren't large enough for a whole kitchen, are normally landfilled by the company. Cover different sections of the kitchen countertop with different types of granite. They'll probably give you a really good price, you'll feel better that you've rescued the beautiful granite from the dump, and you'll end up with a countertop no different from that of some-one who paid full price.

At home, I chose an unusual green granite to complement the plain beech colored cabinets. Usually, the more complex and rare the color, the more expensive the granite.

WOOD. If you choose a wood countertop, consider getting it custom-made by a local craftsman. Purchasing sustainably harvested FSC-certified wood (see chapter 2) is a good option, and having it milled into countertops not only ensures that it's an environmental choice, but it gives you total control over the final look. A craftsman will visit your home, make a template of your kitchen countertop space, and usually either build the counter on-site or partially at his or her workshop.

CONCRETE. While many of us associate concrete with sidewalks or a highway wall, it's a good choice for a kitchen countertop. It's a little bit more complicated than just pouring wet cement into a mold, so have a professional install it. There are three types of concrete countertops:

veined: After the surface is worked, a diamond-impregnated grinding disk zigzags across the slab, revealing marblelike veining in the background. The end result is a very smooth surface equal to that of polished granite. You can have the concrete "burned" with an acid-based wash to make it look like burnished leather.

steel trowel: The smooth, mostly monochromatic surface is notable for its obvious trowel marks and subtle variations of light and dark.

terrazzo: Glass or marble chips worked into the background create a two-toned mottled effect, adding textural interest under the smooth surface. You can even use chips from a set of your own broken antique dishes or collect colorful glass bottles, break them, and have the installer recycle them into your counter.

INDUSTRIAL CHIC

It's hard to beat the design of kitchen supplies and furnishing made for restaurants. A long metal table can handle the daily wear and tear of a family without showing signs of age. Shelves, cabinets, storage bins, and appliances are sold as is, without layers of obnoxious paint, fussy adornment, or packaging. Here less is more: Tough acrylic boxes keep produce fresh, stainless-steel grain bins for flour, slabs of unpolished marble for pastry making. The raw materials look clean and utilitarian.

Soy MILK

Salad MIX

~~vinegar~~

olive oil

Pasta

Watermelon

breAD

WATER

Because my mother does a considerable amount of cooking, it made perfect sense to visit Singer Supply, our local restaurant supply store. The old island was wood laminate, which made it necessary to use a cutting board for chopping vegetables or rolling dough. I replaced it with a waist-high stainless-steel table; the durable metal not only looked nice, but was also so much more versatile than the wood. Best of all, if the table should ever need to be replaced, it can easily be recycled.

When you visit a restaurant supply store, be sure to ask about used equipment. The food service industry is a competitive business, and often those chic stainless stoves, refrigerators, bins, and tables are sold back to the store. For less than half the full price, I was able to purchase industrial equipment for the home that hardly looked used.

ENERGY EFFICIENCY

The kitchen is probably the room in the house that uses the most energy. I can still remember my father complaining that his three children would stand in front of the refrigerator and stare at its contents. What a waste of energy, he must have thought.

Saving energy in the kitchen doesn't mean wrapping layers of insulation around the refrigerator and cooking dinner over an open pit of fire. It's the small things that add up and make a big difference.

First, let's begin with the refrigerator.

With just two coats of chalkboard paint, the front panels of a SubZero refrigerator take on a completely different appearance and purpose. Now I can jot down grocery lists and phone messages.

CONSCIOUS STYLE PROJECT: FRIDGE FACE-LIFT

My parents' large SubZero refrigerator was purchased years before it became fashionable to have restaurant-quality equipment in the home kitchen; my mother wanted it for the extra storage room for her homemade pickled vegetables.

I originally planned to replace it with a large glass-front refrigerator I spied at a local coffee shop. But the more I thought about it, the more impractical it seemed to replace an appliance in perfect condition when its only drawback was cosmetic. The glass-front version, anyway, was extremely loud; even in their large two-story home, the noise would surely be audible even upstairs. The SubZero stayed put.

I decided to cover the front panels, made from removable wood laminate, with two layers of chalkboard paint. Chalkboard paint is different from regular paint; it's a combination of finely ground carbon and talc powder mixed with latex paint. It adheres more easily to a variety of surfaces and is very easy to work with; after two coats of paint, you're almost guaranteed to end up with professional results. I figure a chalkboard fridge would make it easier to keep grocery lists up-to-date and jot down phone messages.

Another way to refinish a refrigerator is to strip off the enamel surface to reveal the natural steel graining underneath. In my Washington, D.C., apartment, I stripped the paint off a rather boring white refrigerator and removed the plastic handles. The end result was a striking stainless-steel appliance that appeared elegant and efficient in the small kitchen.

Stripping a fridge is time intensive, but the end results are worth it. All you need to get started is a bottle of citrus-based paint stripper (an eco-friendly stripper made from citrus ingredients—it's biodegradable and has

(continued)

Conscious Style Project (*continued*)

no dangerous chemicals or fumes), a metal scraper, two small paintbrushes, a tarp, an X-Acto knife, a steel wool pad, and a small can of varnish.

1. Spread a waterproof canvas tarp at the base of the refrigerator. Don't use newspaper; the stripper will leak through and ruin your floor.
2. Carefully score the outside of the refrigerator with the X-Acto knife; the scoring allows the stripper to seep beneath the surface.
3. The next step is to apply the stripper. Pour a small amount of stripper into a glass bowl. Work in sections at a time (freezer door, left side, and so forth) and apply stripper to the first section.
4. Wait until the paint begins to bubble, about twenty` minutes, and use the metal scraper to loosen it. Continue on to other sections until all sections are stripped.
5. When finished, clean with soapy water and remove all traces of stripper; dry with a towel.
6. Once dry, rub the surface with the steel wool; this improves the appearance.
7. Apply a thin layer of varnish to prevent rust; it makes the surface gleam.

Keep it clean. The coils at the back keep the refrigerator from overheating. If they are clogged, they can't function, making the compressor work harder. Every month, unplug the refrigerator, pull it out from the wall, and vacuum the coils clean.

I need my space. Your refrigerator should be at least four inches from the wall.

Keep cool. Don't place your refrigerator near windows, hot water heaters, or warm air from heating ducts, radiators, or the stove. The heat, naturally, makes it harder for the refrigerator to keep your veggies and soy milk cold.

Keep it level. If you're like me, you just let go of the door and walk away, thinking it will shut on its own. It should, but if your refrigerator is not evenly level on the floor, the door won't shut by itself. Imagine the waste!

The stove is another place to save energy:

Size matters. When using smaller pots, use the smaller burner. By using a different size burner, you're saving energy.

Warm up. Thaw frozen food before cooking. A Conscious Style trick: Turn a stainless-steel pan over and place your block of frozen peas on top. The ice will have an immediate reaction to the steel and begin to thaw before your eyes.

Flat surfaces. For electric ranges, use only flat-bottomed pans that make full contact with the burner. Any warped pans are best sent to the scrap yard for recycling.

Keep it clean. The grease plates under the burner must stay *clean*. If you let grease and other gunk build up, the heat won't reflect.

Ovens have varying degrees of energy efficiency:

If you have a choice, choose an electric oven. Gas ovens are inefficient because first, 35 pounds of steel and a large amount of air inside the oven need to be heated before any baking can be done.

At my parents' house, I purchased a convection oven. These reliable ovens use fans to circulate hot air, decreasing the cooking time and generating more even, consistent results.

A few tips:

- Bake the chocolate soufflé in ceramic or glass; these materials outperform metal by allowing you to lower the oven temperature by 25 degrees Fahrenheit.
- Don't cover oven racks with foil—this reduces heat flow and increases cooking time.
- If you have a self-cleaning oven (and it needs to be cleaned), set it to CLEAN after you've already baked something. That way, the oven doesn't have to reheat itself to function properly.

The dishwasher is an eco-friendly convenience—if used properly:

The party is over, and everyone devoured all the fixings you slaved away all day to make. It's late, the last guest has left (*finally!*), and your feet hurt. You turn your head and realize you've got a mountain of dishes, silverware, and cookware sitting in the sink, spilling over to the counter, spilling over to the dining room, spilling over to the family room! Goodness. Should you wash by hand and save water or jam it into your old yet reliable dishwasher and get some shut-eye? Go ahead and let technology work for you.

If you have a dishwasher, run it only when it's full and don't rinse your dishes before putting them in. If you have an energy-saving option, use it and skip the dry cycle; after the dishes have been washed, simply open the door and the hot steamy air will evaporate off the plates (and you'll get a mini-facial).

I replaced the dishwasher in my parents' house with a Swedish (gotta love the Swedes) dishwasher that uses only 4 gallons of water per cycle; compare that to the 10 gallons our old dishwasher needed.

The dishwasher is from Asko, founded by a Swedish farmer named Karl-Erik Andersson who set out to build his mother a better washing machine. Asko's dishwasher uses 40 percent less electricity, and its inner casings are superdurable (dishwashers are notorious for breaking down) and are made from surgical-quality stainless steel. And for those who like to meditate in the kitchen, it's triple-insulated, which means it's always whisper-quiet when scrubbing that goulash from your pots and pans.

SETTING THE TABLE

If you're like me, you follow the mantra "You are what you eat" and nourish your body with healthful, delicious food. Whenever I have friends over for dinner, I like the challenge of proving that vegetarian cuisine doesn't mean tofu and sprouts; even the die-hard carnivores are surprised to learn my sweet and sour "chicken" (made from soy) and veggie burgers taste good and are healthy, too.

When I have friends over, I'm also very particular about what types of tableware I choose. A large white dinner plate makes pasta with pesto look so good by highlighting every little tear of cilantro sprinkled along the edges. A late-19th-century French café au lait cup turns coffee-drinking into an *experience*. A bamboo placemat adds a new dimension to the table and keeps those drips of tomato bisque from spotting your linens.

Eco-friendly tableware used to be unattractive and strange—one piece I discovered was a biodegradable fork you couldn't get wet. *Please*. But on one sunny Saturday afternoon, I walked through the SoHo area of New York City and discovered small shops and big-name chain stores selling beautiful tableware pieces made from hand-turned wood discards, recycled glass, and natural materials. Suddenly, Conscious Style tableware was everywhere.

RECYCLED GLASS. Have you ever wondered what happens to the empty glass jars and bottles you set aside for recycling? Since glass can be recycled infinitely, most of your jars get made into food containers again. But a lucky few get made into hand-poured recycled glass tableware.

Bottles, jars, and even old windowpanes are collected, sorted, washed, and then shattered into tiny pieces. After colorants are added, the glass mixture is fed into a hot furnace, where it cooks for several hours at temperatures up to 2,400 degrees Fahrenheit. From there, the molten glass is poured into molds, pressed, and cooled.

Recycled glassware is different in appearance from conventional pieces. Because using recycled glass isn't an exact science (the chemical formulation of glass is different from piece to piece), the end results can be unpredictable. But that's exactly what makes recycled glassware so desirable; the air bubbles (formed by natural gases during the molding process), color, and texture give each piece an organic shape and feel.

The majority of recycled glassware is made in Spain and Mexico and can usually be identified by its celery green color and abundance of air bubbles. The pieces are inexpensive and durable enough for everyday use—they can even go through the dishwasher. You probably have a few pieces in your kitchen and didn't even know they were recycled.

Another form of glass recycling doesn't involve hot molten glass at all. GreenGlass was founded by three South African entrepreneurs who realized they could cut a wine bottle in half, flip the two pieces around, fuse them together, polish the edges, and create attractive drinking cups. The design is intentional, highlighting the

A grouping of roadside weeds—Queen Anne's lace and goldenrod—looks refined on the dining room table, sitting in a collection of old trophies. The glasses are made from recycled glass by a South African company called GreenGlass.

indentations and designs found on fine wine bottles. These clever cups—which include tumblers, wineglasses, and champagne flutes—have found a celebrity following, gracing the tables of the king of Spain and actor Robert Redford.

WOOD. If given a pile of wood and told to do something with it, most of us would simply start a fire. But if you're Vermont wood-worker Luke Mann, you create handturned wood bowls.

Salvaging wood from trees that fell after storms or logging site discards, Mann uses a wood lathe to produce turnings that "are pleasing to the eye and to the touch, with a surface that improves with time and use." The natural knots, graining, and distortion add beauty to the pieces, accentuating the shape, color, and thickness. Designer Gabriela Valenzuela, who makes wood bowls and accessories from naturally fallen rain-forest trees and driftwood, says wood bowls "call us back to the elemental appreciation for nature in its purest forms."

Wood bowls are especially useful in the kitchen. They work well, and pieces can be fully utilitarian—handy when mixing batter, emulsifying salad dressings, or tossing salads—or decorative serving pieces. And by collecting handmade wood bowls, you're purchasing an original creation and supporting the arts community.

To keep your wood bowls in shape, Mann recommends washing them with a mild soap and occasionally applying walnut or canola oil.

VINTAGE AND FLEA MARKET FINDS. It seems that everyone has more tableware pieces than they really need. Our cabinets, pantry, and cupboards are overflowing with dishes, chargers, cups and saucers, and an infinite number of pieces we're not quite sure what to do with. No wonder flea markets, thrift shops, and antique stores are brimming with vintage dishes, bowls, serving pieces, and flatware. But if you've been eating off paper plates lately, maybe it's time to scavenge for preowned pieces that are unusual, beautiful, unique, and often sold at bargain basement prices.

You probably won't find complete sets with matching utensils, which is perfectly fine. Instead, mix and match your pieces. Keep color combinations in mind, and match pieces based on your own personal taste. An antique white tureen, matched with modern white plates and a "set" of assorted sterling silver flatware works because the colors don't clash even if the patterns differ.

When you've found a set of crystal goblets or sterling silver flatware at a tag sale or flea market, it's easy to bring them back to life and maintain their good looks. Some Conscious Style tips:

- Don't overload the dishwasher. Dishes should not touch each other, since the clanging and clinking can cause dents, scratches, and breaks.
- It's safe to put fine china dinnerware in the dishwasher. Use a mild detergent and the lightest setting possible. If the china has a gold or platinum band, wash it by hand, since the extreme heat of any cycle will discolor the metal.
- When drying any delicate dinnerware, use the energy-saving drying setting to avoid exposing the pieces to extremely high heat.
- Wash crystal by hand; the jets in the dishwasher can break the glasses. When washing by hand, add a little bit of white vinegar to a tub of lukewarm water when rinsing the glasses; this will prevent spotting.
- Don't wash sterling silver or silverplate flatware with stainless steel. When the two metals touch, a chemical reaction dulls the finish on the silver pieces.
- If a decanter has red wine stains, simply fill the decanter with warm water, detergent, and a spoonful of rice. Shake thoroughly.
- If the stopper on a decanter is stuck, wrap the neck with a small hot towel. The glass will expand and release the stopper.

CHAPTER FOUR

FURNITURE

If woman's place is in the home, why am I always in my car?

—ANONYMOUS

In the last decade, buying furniture has evolved from a mind-boggling, time-consuming experience into a streamlined, and—dare I say—fun way to spend the weekend. Gone are the days of snooty stores whose rude salespeople sold overpriced tables, chairs, and beds. No longer do we need to wait months for a dining room table to be delivered; today we can pick a table from the showroom and have it loaded into the car. We can even go online and have a sofa delivered to our house in days—custom-made in the fabric of our choice. And we don't have to settle for furniture made from endangered woods or leather sofas from the hides of cows; furniture made from sustainably harvested wood and cow-friendly faux suede chairs (that feel just as soft as real suede) are everywhere: at the mall, in catalogs, and online.

But before you go to the mall or antiques store and look for that chair or table, glance around your own house first and reuse what you already own. You could detach, for example, a mirror from a dresser, paint it white, add hooks and wire on the back, and hang it above the sink in the bathroom. Break up a bedroom set (which

LEFT: Citrus-based paint stripper makes refinishing metal furniture a lot easier. BELOW: A wood table I picked up at a junk store is a charming addition to the living room.

Vintage metal and wood chairs can be used indoors or outdoors to create a rustic, homey feeling.

looks too rigidly coordinated anyway) and use the nightstand in the family room or the dresser in the dining room to hold linens and cutlery. When I added new chairs to the kitchen, I took the old wooden ones, painted them green, distressed them a bit with sandpaper, and used them as outdoor chairs.

But if you've searched high and low in your home, come up empty-handed, and have decided to buy a new piece, remember my golden rule about furniture: These purchases should last you a lifetime, so a little planning and homework will pay off in the end.

A few considerations:

1. Don't buy based on price alone. Since furniture should last a lifetime, better quality will mean a better investment.
2. Good craftsmanship matters. Pull the drawers out of a nightstand or dresser, and examine the joints for tightness. The more seamless the fit, the better. Also, just because a piece is an antique, don't overlook major flaws; a bureau that can't hold your clothes because the wood is rotting isn't a good buy.
3. Don't overestimate your space. It's easy to end up with way too much furniture in a room. Before buying an end table, determine if you really need it. Your furniture should complement the room, not make it busier to the eye.
4. Squeeze the arms of the sofa to feel for adequate padding; look at the stitching carefully and look for frays or overly taut areas. Don't be afraid to put the sofa on its side in the store to examine the bottom.
5. Look for cracks, bubbles, or discoloration in wood finishes. And bring a small white towel with you to the flea market or antique store; rub it across the surface of a wood piece and see if any brown smudges come up. If so, the piece has been covered with shoe polish to temporarily hide damage. It doesn't necessarily mean the piece is bad, but be aware of any defects before purchase.
6. Avoid looking at home design magazines before shopping. Choose pieces that appeal to you, not what's "in" at the

moment. What's trendy today may not be the fashion in a few years.

One of the biggest hurdles I needed to overcome with my mother was her aversion to vintage and antique furniture. She'd ask, Why buy something that's been *used*? She thought I was crazy for loading a rusty washtub I found on the side of the road into the back of the car. And there was no way, she proclaimed, that it would ever end up in her house no matter how much time I spent "refurbishing" it. There was no way, I proclaimed, that it *wouldn't* end up in the home no matter how much time she spent "rejecting" it.

But when she saw that my purchases ranged from brand-new pieces to vintage furniture from the 1950s, she realized the whole house wouldn't be filled with roadside discoveries. Just because you had an old piece of furniture, I explained, it didn't mean the whole room had to look like an indoor flea market. On the contrary, by mixing and matching the new with the old, the different textures and designs "worked" in her mind. Who would've thought an old clock from a watch repair store would look so perfect in the kitchen? Or that recovering a sofa in Polish hemp fabric would look so nice?

FACE-LIFT

A sofa is a purchase that should last you forever. I don't believe in buying a sofa with the intention of replacing it in a few years. A cheap sofa may look good the first year, but after its first anniversary, inexpensive fabric pulls, cushions feel uneven, and springs have, well, sprung. A good sofa may have a higher price tag, but you'll come out on top down the road for making the smart investment.

But the day will arrive when the family cat thinks the armrest is a scratching post or the kids (and possibly you) can't resist jumping up and down on the cushions. Fabric will get torn, stains will inevitably occur, and padding will get compacted. This loyal member of the family has seen holidays, birthdays, and movie marathons, so don't toss it to the curb—reupholster it.

Reupholstering a sofa does more than replace worn-out fabric.

You can change the shape of the sofa by removing or adding padding, replace synthetic materials with healthy all-natural ones, and create a new decorating scheme simply based on what fabric you choose for the exterior. It's not expensive to do. Changing an orange velvet sofa to monochromatic canvas is like getting a brand-new sofa for half the price. Reupholstery is not only an environmental option, it's an economical choice.

When I decided to redo the sofa in the family room and change it from an overstuffed gray sofa into something more sophisticated, I first considered exactly what my options were. I didn't choose the upholsterer that provided the lowest price, but the one I felt—based solely on my own intuition—would do the best job. I met with the upholsterers separately and asked for their opinions on what to do with the sofa, asked about their work history, and asked if they would object to my visiting their studio. Second, I decided to provide my own fabric, which reduced the cost of the job significantly. For strength and color, I chose a heavyweight all-hemp fabric made in Poland; I liked the natural brown color and tight weave of the fabric. I also decided to remove the back cushions altogether (which also lowered the price); instead, I replaced them with premade oversize square pillows (stuffed with synthetic down) to give the sofa a more inviting look.

When reupholstering a sofa, a few considerations:

1. You can always bring your own fabric. Because most upholsterers (look under *upholstery* in the yellow pages) do not carry eco-friendly fabrics like organic cotton or hemp, you can supply your own. Be sure to order enough material (the upholsterer can tell you how much to order), and make sure the estimate is adjusted. You're also free to purchase bolts of vintage or antique fabric. I purchased several yards of 1890s French ticking (which was only $20 a yard) and reupholstered two flea market footstools with it.

2. Choose all-cotton padding. Most sofas use synthetic cotton for interior padding to save money. Ask for 100 percent real

cotton. Cotton is a natural material, so it won't release harmful gases into your home over time.

3. Reupholster other pieces. Have an ottoman, the dining room chairs, or a side chair reupholstered in the same fabric. Order extra fabric and put in a "group order" with the upholsterer. This should save you money and will help coordinate pieces in the room.

4. Take any fabric remnants with you. Leftover fabric can be used to make pillows and tablecloths, or recover the seat cushion of a chair. And here's a do-it-yourself project: Take an old office memo corkboard, remove the frame, and cover it with the leftover fabric. Secure the fabric to the back of the board with a staple gun, add hooks to the back, and hang it in the kitchen or by your desk. You're not only recycling leftover fabric, but bringing design consistency to two separate rooms.

Another idea is to use slipcovers. In the past, slipcovers were only available in a limited variety of fabrics and the promise that one-size-fits-all wasn't always true. Today is quite different. In the lobby of the Paramount Hotel in New York City, a modern boutique-style hotel nestled in the heart of Times Square, metal chairs are covered with white slipcovers for beauty and practicality. If a slipcover gets stained, it can be easily removed and washed. At home, you can cover a chair with white terry cloth for the bathroom or with white canvas for the home office. Either way, you're giving a chair a second chance while adding a dose of modernity to the room.

WOOD FURNITURE

A lot of us feel guilty when buying a new piece of wood furniture. We know the piece came directly from a tree, which was probably from a clear-cut forest. But there's no reason to feel guilty; you can have beautiful wood furniture and still do the right thing.

In general, avoid wood furniture if you don't know its source. The

Framed family pictures are an inexpensive way to add interest to your walls. Here, unmatched frames are hung in an interesting pattern; a level and artists' tacks guarantee professional results.

majority of furniture—especially tropical woods like mahogany and teak—is from clear-cut forests where logging ruins the natural biodiversity of the forest.

But if there is one good thing those horrific six-o'clock-news pictures of clear-cut ancient forests and rain forests have done, it's to raise consciousness and boost something called plantation-grown wood. A growing number of businesses now manufacture furniture made from woods that aren't from forests, but from well-managed farms with the sole purpose of raising trees for lumber.

Gardening retailer Smith & Hawken sells plantation-grown teak furniture through its catalog, Web site, and chain of stores. It doesn't use teak cut down from forests. The wood is harvested from decades-old tree plantations on the island of Java. Smith & Hawken was one of the first retailers to use truly sustainable harvested teak.

Sustainable teak furniture is a good investment. In colonial times, teak was used for shipbuilding because of its density and imperviousness to rotting, splitting, and buckling. A teak chair purchased today will likely last for a century—even if left outdoors. Over time, teak will take on a warm gray patina, reminiscent of the benches seen in parks throughout England. In India, teak furniture that is over two hundred years old is common.

Aside from Smith & Hawken, you can find sustainably harvested tropical woods in unexpected places. IKEA, for example, manufactures furniture made from rubberwood grown on plantations; in the past, when rubber trees were no longer tapped, they were simply burned. At a furniture outlet store in Morgantown, Pennsylvania, I purchased a handmade mahogany trunk and matching chair made from plantation-grown mahogany. The dark grain adds a handsome touch to the family room, and it makes me feel better because I did not contribute to the decline of the rain forests when I purchased them. In Australia, 45 percent of all lumber—a wide variety of soft and hard woods—comes from plantation farms. It's just a matter of time before furniture that *isn't* plantation grown will need to be identified.

Another benefit of buying plantation-grown wood furniture is that it has also been identified as a significant strategy for reducing carbon dioxide concentrations. Scientists in Australia found that the young trees on plantation farms absorb more carbon dioxide from the atmosphere than older forests; plantation forests are therefore helping to combat the greenhouse effect.

> Just because you have an old piece of furniture, I explained, it didn't mean the whole room had to look like an indoor flea market.

Another alternative is to purchase furniture made from reclaimed timber. Large wood planks rescued from farmhouses, broken tables, and abandoned warehouses are sometimes hundreds of years old. The rich color, warmth, and charm of this wood make for perfect furniture. One company, Conklins Authentic Antique Barnwood of Susquehanna, Pennsylvania, has a motto: "After 150 years of wind, rain, and sun, they're ready for a new life." And that naturally aged wood—full of knots, nicks, and charming flaws—is remilled into beautiful wood furniture like beds, dressers, benches, and tables. The key to buying reclaimed timber furniture is to not outfit an entire room with it. (If you do that, it will look like you tore down a farmhouse and built furniture.) Instead, be selective and buy a long farmhouse table and pair it with a set of galvanized steel chairs.

In general, when buying wood furniture, ask questions. Stores and salespeople are a lot more knowledgeable today than just a few years ago. They can tell you the source of the wood and even the glues used to bind the wood veneer. And if they don't know, the manufacturer can you tell you exactly the information that you need. Read tags—I never would have known the mahogany furniture was actually plantation grown if I hadn't stopped to read the colorful tag.

VINTAGE WOOD

Most people when they think of antique wood furniture, envision centuries-old pieces with sky-high price tags to match. But there's no need to visit Sotheby's to buy a piece of history when you can buy vintage wood furniture. Vintage wood ranges from the early 20th century Arts and Crafts movement—a rejection of the Victorian excess design philosophy—to utilitarian pieces dating from as late as the 1970s. Another reason to buy vintage over new: You can own wood pieces made with rare woods without feeling bad; you're recycling.

Vintage wood is also affordable. I found a mission-style desk at a nearby flea market for just $50. It's not a valuable piece of furniture, and it certainly does not need to be appraised, but its aged finish and exposed construction details add historical charm to the room. Like famed architect Frank Lloyd Wright, who believed that furniture should complement the architecture of a home, I've always believed it's important to mix and match new pieces with old. That way, you create an environment devoid of the "catalog look" and create a living space that is all your own and evokes charm, character, and personality.

The best places to buy vintage wood are at flea markets, yard sales, antique stores, junk stores, and even online. When surfing the World Wide Web for furniture, you'll find thousands of Web sites that sell vintage pieces—from furniture to lighting—at reasonable prices. The Internet is especially useful for completing a set; if you find a set of three Stickley chairs in an antique store and need a fourth, you can surf the Web for the missing piece.

Some of the better-known vintage wood manufacturers to look for are Stickley, Frank Lloyd Wright, Herman Miller, Gilbert Rhode, and Heywood-Wakefield. These pieces are highly collectible and can be expensive. But for every Stickley chair, there are dozens of lesser-known manufacturers that made beautiful pieces in the same style, and they are more affordable and easier to find.

For the family room, I purchased a rocking chair and an armchair. I found them at a nearby junk store and bought them because I liked the organic, rustic look. It was only after I found a barely legible paper

This galvanized washtub was found at a junk store with a piece of paper attached to it that said FREE. With drainage holes on the bottom, it is perfect as an outdoor bar, keeping refreshments icy cold. All the glassware is made from 100 percent recycled glass.

label on the bottom of one chair that I learned it was made by the HC Dexter Chair Company, a furniture manufacturer from the Arts and Crafts movement. A little bit more research revealed that pieces from the company are collectible and that there was even an exhibition of pieces from the company in a museum in upstate New York.

When shopping for vintage wood, your eye is the best judge of what is real and what is fake. Fortunately, because many of these pieces were made in the 20th century, the market hasn't been flooded with fakes (as so often seen with early 18th- and 19th-century antiques). So when you find a piece that looks like Heywood-Wakefield—with its blond wood surface and modern design that makes it seem to float just above the floor—it probably is the genuine article.

And here's a Conscious Style tip: If the wood furniture has small dents in it, simply place a few layers of cloth over the dent and run a hot iron over it. The heat will make the dents swell back into their original position. And the richness of the wood can be brought to life with a simple vegetable oil polish. (See chapter 10 for the recipe.)

METAL

Metal furniture has a bad reputation. While wood may be described as warm and homey, metal is often described as cold or sterile.

I've always had a fascination with metal furniture. A simple iron table, free of added ornamentation or color, serves as a desk in my apartment; its thin legs make it look light and airy but strong and substantial at the same time. A stripped metal filing cabinet looks like a piece of art; instead of having it near my desk, it serves double-duty as a nightstand in my bedroom and complements my walnut mission bed. At my parents' house, I bought a stainless-steel cart at a restaurant supply store and put a TV on top and the VCR and DVD player on the lower shelves; now the TV isn't a fixed presence in the room—it can easily be wheeled away.

Real office supply stores—not those chain stores, but the retailers that provide desks, chairs, and filing cabinets to corporations—are good places to shop. While it may seem odd to have a metal office desk at home, when you pair it with an antique wood chair, the look works. The juxtaposition makes a utilitarian-meets-comfort statement. And for an added touch, you can get any metal furniture powder-coated in the color of your choice; auto body shops and metal refinishers are good places to contact for such a job.

There are several reasons to consider metal. First, it adds another textural element to the room. Second, metal is durable, timeless in appeal, and often very light in weight (aluminum furniture especially). And here's my favorite reason: Metal is fully recyclable. I always look for metal furniture free of any plastic or wood parts. It's easier to recycle.

SACRILEGIOUS CHIC

How many times have you wondered what to do with your TV? If you're like most people, you prop it up somewhere or simply throw your hands into the air and buy a cheap TV stand at a discount retailer.

Finding a place for my TV was just one problem solved by my use of unwanted religious furniture and accessories. In one of my favorite stores in Washington, D.C., Good Wood, I purchased a wood podium that I thought would be perfect to hold a TV in my apartment. I didn't realize it was also an old church podium, probably just a few decades young and used in a church where the Sunday sermon was delivered. Behind the elaborate front was a hollow back, with shelves, which made it a perfect place to store unsightly electronic equipment—my VCR, stereo, and a mountain of wires—and a small collection of tapes. When I added wheels to the bottom, it could easily be moved for use in different rooms, too. Problem solved!

Old church furniture and accessories may seem odd or even sacrilegious to you. But they shouldn't. Lots of churches are releasing

The elegant TV stand was once used as a podium in a church. There are shelves in the back, which I use to store electronic equipment, tapes, and a pile of wires. I purchased the antique pottery on my book tour in South Korea.

unwanted pieces to vintage and antique stores for resale; the religious institution benefits because it receives a cut of the sale for its association. The buyer benefits because he or she acquires something different that is well built, functional, and decorative.

A long wood pew would work well in a hallway: Store shoes underneath, stack blankets at one end, and sit and enjoy a favorite book. Wall sconces (I have two metal ones) can hang like artwork on the wall and serve a function by holding large pillar candles or an arrangement of flowers. And that podium can be used as an entertainment center or pushed up against a wall to display cherished items.

If your local used furniture or antique store doesn't sell church furniture and accessories, you can place a request with the buyer to look for it. Don't go to a church and make an offer. A quick tip: Use religious artifacts sparingly. Own too many, and it'll look like you've robbed the Sistine Chapel.

BUYING NEW

Wouldn't it be great to walk into your favorite furniture store, pick out a sofa or ottoman that you like, and be able to get the store to custom upholster it in hemp or organic cotton ticking? Or to ask the salesperson if the wood veneer was put together with formaldehyde-free glue? Well, you can.

When did furniture shopping become so convenient? Because of fierce competition between stores, retailers are doing everything possible to get your sale.

UPHOLSTERY

Do your homework ahead of time: Find fabric retailers that sell eco-friendly fabrics like hemp, organic cotton, Ultraleather, and Ultrasuede. Ask for samples (if they charge a nominal fee for samples, most will refund the money when you order), and bring them with you to the store. After ordering the chair, contact the fabric retailer and have the requested amount of fabric shipped *directly* to the furniture store or the factory where the piece will be made. This way, you can avoid the hassle of having to transport a heavy bolt of fabric yourself, and you'll save money on shipping. In a few weeks, you'll have the chair of your dreams.

DO-IT-YOURSELF

A good thing to look for is unfinished furniture, like simple bed frames, tables, and chairs. Leave the more complicated wood items, like dressers and armoires, to the pros, and don't attempt to finish them yourself. By going au naturel with your furniture, you can use a vegetable-based stain or paint the furniture with VOC-free enamel to get the look you want without adding harmful toxins to the atmosphere. If your pieces aren't going to be exposed to the elements or to daily use, you can even leave them unfinished.

GLUE

Formaldehyde is a gas that has proved to be the cause of health problems. Scientists who work with large amounts of form-aldehyde go to great lengths to protect themselves from expo-sure. But did you know that formaldehyde can be found right in most homes?

Formaldehyde is used in ad-hesives, paints, varnishes, and textiles, so read all labels and look for formaldehyde-free ma-terials for your home. When buying wood furniture, find out what type of glue was used to bind the wood together; the Conscious Style choice is simple white glue. (Yes, that's the same glue you used as a child.) If

CONSCIOUS STYLE PROFILE: AZCAST DESIGN

When you see a pile of plane, train, and automotive parts, do you (a) see junk, (b) think of the movie *Planes, Trains & Automobiles*, or (c) see a bottle opener, chair, and dining room table?

If you're Eyreick Williamson, the answer is c.

As a child, Williamson grew up at a foundry, at his father's side, learning about the casting process and loving the noise of grinding machinery, the smell of molten metal, and the raw energy of the plant. Tired of running a company that made parts for a furniture manufacturer, Williamson had an idea. "I realized I could make beautiful furniture from recycled metal." The staunch environmentalist and artisan discussed his idea with five other artists in the Los Angeles, California, area, bought an abandoned foundry in City of Industry, California (located on the outskirts of L.A.), and launched Azcast Products in 1994.

He describes his company's design philosophy as "highly functional and useful." He says, "I try not to design anything that sits on someone's table and collects dust. I want people to buy our products and use them." Citing the Heywood-Wakefield furniture company—a company that manufac-tured simple maple furniture in the 1940s and 1950s—as a design influ-ence, Williamson produces furniture, tableware, and bathroom accessories that are straightforward and simple in design. Nothing is "exaggerated in design that attracts attention to itself. I want people to look at my pieces and have it be pleasing to the eye." Everything from a whimsical bottle opener in the shape of squirrel, a "recurve" 100 percent recycled chair made from recycled aluminum, and unusual materials like Environ, a hard 100 percent recycled resin material used as seating for some of Azcast's chairs, become part of the company's product line.

(continued)

One of Azcast's first products was a vase in the shape of an aluminum milk bottle. "That piece really put us on the map," said Williamson. The product was such a huge hit that knock-offs were quickly made overseas by other manufacturers—who, unlike Azcast, didn't use recycled metal. But unlike other competitors, who might quickly outsource their work overseas to compete, Williamson refused to send work to overseas factories where workers earn low wages. But if you think that higher prices mean he's losing customers, think again; Azcast's customers seem happy to pay a little bit more for his pieces because they know that they are doing the right thing.

So just how important is it for Williamson to use recycled materials? "I saw an opportunity to create a company that made great products using recycled materials," he says. But Azcast Products does more than take scrap aluminum and make vases and tables with it. By following the adage "less is more" Williamson personally oversees the design process of every product Azcast creates. "I see materials going into products when it's not even needed." By keeping all their products true to their origins, legs of chairs or tables are never painted, but rather polished or left raw for a matte finish. You also won't find plastic hinges or brackets on the company's accessories or materials added simply for ornamentation. This careful guidance by Williamson, this "truth in materials," helps to keep unnecessary products from being used.

But first and foremost, Williamson hopes people buy his products not just because they are eco-friendly, but because "the look of the pieces catches their eye." Says Williamson, "When people find out our products are eco-friendly, they get really excited about it. It makes them feel a little bit better that some mahogany tree wasn't cut down in Honduras somewhere." And it doesn't hurt that the metal bar stool looks so good, too.

another glue was used, ask what levels of formaldehyde are in it; according to IKEA, the German E1 and Finnish regulations outline the strictest requirements for formaldehyde use anywhere in the world. Consider furniture that abides by these regulations to be ideal.

NEW MATERIALS

Forget teak, steel, and antiques. This is the 21st century: Space-age materials and old favorites—once cast off as tacky—are making a comeback.

ULTRASUEDE

When you want a leather club chair or a chrome ottoman covered in suede, go fake. Ultrasuede and Ultraleather are the most practical choice when upholstering a sofa, chair, or ottoman when you want the leather look. Made entirely from polyester microfiber, Ultrasuede and Ultraleather look good, come in hundreds of colors, and are easy to maintain. They can be treated with a stain-resistant spray, so if someone spills a drink on the material, the liquid will bead up so you can clean it with a towel.

TREETAP

Perhaps the only luxury item that actually helps preserve the rain forests, Treetap is a rubber collected in the heart of the Amazon rain forest. Collected by indigenous tribes that tap rubber trees (this doesn't hurt the tree or forest), a wild latex is gathered, poured over old canvas sacks, and cured over an open fire. The leathery, strong material is a good choice for areas exposed to the elements or prone to spills. Here's a Conscious Style tip: Before covering furniture with Treetap (I covered a small footstool with it), cut the material you'll need, and fold, bend, crease, and twist it until the material softens and begins to form small cracks on the surface. This will give the material a distressed look that simulates the appearance of antique leather.

AIR

We all remember the psychedelic furniture of the '60s and '70s: bean bag chairs, shag carpet, and air-filled vinyl pillows. There are new chairs and sofas filled with air—which only uses one-sixth of the resources needed to produce traditional seating. But if the thought of huffing and puffing into a plastic pillow sounds daunting, don't worry. Instead of using a bike pump or your lungs, all you have to do is plug in a hair dryer to fill up the furniture.

RECYCLED METAL

One day it's a trash can, the next day a part in a car, and tomorrow a limited-edition coffee table. The cost of recycled metal ore has dropped significantly over the years, leading more furniture designers to use it in their designs. Recycled metal lends a silvery chic to furniture and is more often found in modern designs; when sand-cast and left unpainted, it has an organic raw finish. When polished, the finish is shiny and luminous.

CHAPTER FIVE

SANCTUARY

Life is something that happens when you can't get to sleep.

—FRAN LEBOWITZ

Are you among the millions of people who have trouble sleeping? Often, the problem lies with the bed itself—most beds (sheets, pillows, and mattresses) are made of artificial foams, formaldehyde, fluorocarbons, and synthetic fibers that produce gases or fumes.

Since in a year you'll spend 2,920 hours sleeping, your bed should be the healthiest place in your home. But if it's like most, it's made of synthetic materials that over time lose their shape, become ergonomically unsound, and emit toxic fumes. It's no wonder your bed affects your sleep, your back, and your health. If you sleep poorly, or if you care about what you breathe as you sleep, consider creating a *Conscious Style* serenity bed.

THE FOUNDATION

Before you begin buying sheets and pillows, you must choose the most crucial item—the bed itself. The Conscious Style approach toward buying a bed is simple: Don't buy new—use what you have or shop at flea markets, thrift shops, or secondhand stores. Buying

LEFT: Today, it's easy to find synthetic down pillows and duvets that are as fluffy as the real thing. BELOW: These pillows are covered in soft chambray and filled with fluffy recycled plastic.

Organic cotton sheets have come a long way. Today they are made with high-thread counts and availale in a wide variety of colors.

old isn't just acquiring something previously used, it's getting a piece of furniture with a lived-in look that can't be replicated at a furniture store. The charm and eclectic look will help define the personality of the bedroom, rebelling against bedroom "sets" and giving the room personality and a look all its own.

When looking for a bed, visit flea markets, antiques malls, estate sales, tag sales, church bazaars, and even a roadside curb during spring cleanup in your neighborhood. Don't forget to look at your current bed; maybe a coat of paint would bring it back to life. First, look beyond the color of the bed and focus on its condition. Is it in good shape? If it needs to be repaired, can you (and I emphasize the word *you*) easily fix it? Will the bed fit in your bedroom? Is the size standard to common mattress sizes? (Antique beds are usually not standard sizes and will require resizing by a professional, which can be expensive, so consider your budget before a purchase.) When you find a bed that you like, trust your instinct and buy it. Don't waste your time hunting for the perfect bed—save yourself the time and go for it.

Any bed can be brought back to life (despite its layers of avocado green paint or dark wood veneer) with a little sandpaper and paint. There's no need to strip metal or wood furniture to its base; just lightly sand it by hand, add a coat of primer, and paint it with a high gloss enamel paint. Take a break from the basic Conscious Style colors—white, khaki, navy—and use a bold color to paint the bed. Don't be afraid to paint the frame with nautical orange, forest green, or basic black. Small doses of powerful color in a modest room are powerful but not overpowering. White sheets and dark wood floors look great with a metal bed painted glossy tangerine.

You can also apply a citrus stripper to the bed and haphazardly remove different layers of paint. By not stripping the bed entirely, you'll leave some remnants of paint—perhaps a spot of green here, a little bit of red there. Some paint that isn't scraped off will crackle naturally. The end result is a bed reminiscent of old farmhouse pieces.

Finally, fight the impulse to match the color of your bed with other pieces of furniture or accessories. For example, if you paint the bed a light green, paint the dresser a neutral color and leave the bedside table unfinished. By doing so, you'll avoid putting together a room that is too rigidly coordinated.

SLEEP LIKE A BABY

Once you've picked out a bed, it's time to purchase a mattress. This is not the place to cut corners; buy the finest quality mattress you can afford. An inexpensive mattress will not last long, is most likely made from synthetic materials, and will need to be dumped in just a few years. Considering that we spend a third of our lives sleeping in bed, paying a little more for quality materials is a wise investment.

Most major brand mattresses cover their innerspring units with unhealthy petroleum products that can cause a host of medical and sleep-related problems. These unnatural materials are perfect breeding grounds for bacteria, mold and mildew, and dust mites (a microscopic member of the spider family that thrives in the dust). Buying a mattress made with natural materials will significantly help allergy sufferers.

Having a mattress custom-made sounds like a luxury for the rich, but it's something within anyone's reach and is worth the extra time and effort. While you may not be able to pick up the phone and have an all-natural mattress delivered the very same day, once your mattress arrives your body will thank you.

- Choose a mattress made from 100 percent natural cotton padding (which helps skin breathe comfortably), cotton batting (instead of horsehair or lamb's wool), or latex foam (a natural foam made from the rubber tree; cheaper mattresses use a synthetic foam that, over time, releases toxic gases). Finally, select a mattress that is guaranteed to be completely formaldehyde free.

- Ask for hand-tufting; 40 to 60 tufts (depending on size) provide better back support and keep layered cotton batting from shifting.
- Cover the mattress in the fabric, or ticking, of your choice. Foxfibre, for example, is an organic cotton material made without the use of harmful dyes. Foxfibre is grown from seeds that are bred to grow naturally in many different colors, usually in shades of green and reddish brown. Color-grown cotton does not need bleaching or dyeing to achieve the color, so no harmful dyes are expelled into water.

   Another good choice is hemp. Naturally mildew resistant and breathable, it is an ideal fiber for bedding. While it may cost more than cotton, it is three times stronger and twice as resistant to abrasion.

No matter what mattress you sleep on, make sure it comes with at least a fifteen year guarantee. That, in itself, should help you sleep a little better.

HEAD REST: CHOOSING A PILLOW

It's the little things that turn your bed into an enchanting sanctuary: warm lighting, soft sheets, an old mirror hung just so. But it's the right pillow—not too soft, not too firm—that can help you to totally, completely relax.

The only way to pick the right pillow is to try a few out for yourself. One by one. To choose a pillow that's not too soft or hard, lay your head on the pillow. If your head has enough support and doesn't sink to the bottom, it's just right.

Use common sense. If you throw pillows on the floor before calling it a night, you have too many pillows. For a full-size bed, all you need are two standard-size pillows; for larger beds, I like two standard and two Euro-size pillows.

Also, while feather down may seem like the most natural and comfortable option, it is not a good Conscious Style choice. Down

Eco-friendly furniture doesn't always mean it'll cost more. This armoire, made from plantation-grown mahogany, cost only a third of what a traditional piece would cost. Inside, vintage pieces and new organic cotton sheets are neatly stacked.

is the soft underfeathering plucked out of live geese to supply filling for products such as comforters, pillows, and ski parkas.

Plucking the geese causes them considerable pain and distress. Four or five times in their lives, they will squirm as a plucker tears out five ounces of their feathers. After the last plucking, the geese have five weeks to grow more feathers before they are sent through a machine that plucks their longest feathers. From there they go to the slaughterhouse.

Apart from the cruelty involved in its production, down has its drawbacks as a cold-weather insulator that synthetic insulators do not have. Not only is down expensive, it also loses its insulating ability when wet, whereas you can clean a synthetic down pillow in the washing machine.

Here are some good filling materials to look for:

- Primaloft. Engineered to mimic the look and feel of down, Primaloft fill represents a new standard in allergy relief. With their warmth and fluffiness, these special high-loft, micro-cluster fibers behave ounce for ounce exactly like down with one notable exception: They're 100 percent free of unhealthy allergens and designed to stay that way.
- Buckwheat hulls. On a trip to a Buddhist retreat in the California wilderness, I discovered the comfort of a Japanese buckwheat pillow. The small buckwheat hulls shift inside the case to match the exact contour of your neck and head. Buckwheat hulls don't conduct heat, and they help maintain a perfect body temperature all night. Look for pillows filled with 100 percent pesticide-free hulls.
- GreenCotton. Cotton that is not bleached with chlorine, dyed, or treated with chemicals such as formaldehyde is usually softer than regular processed cotton because it has not been stripped of its natural properties by chemical treatments. Buy cotton filling labeled unbleached or a brand-name filling called GreenCotton.
- EcoSpun: At first glance, it could look like any other ordinary pillow. But on the inside, there's a big difference: The

pillow is generously stuffed with a fleecelike material made from 100 percent recycled plastic soda bottles. EcoSpun is strong, shrink-resistant, and completely hypoallergenic.

THE COMFORT ZONE

Sweet dreams are inevitable when you surround your body with soft sheets and a large, fluffy comforter.

Begin with a comforter filled with synthetic down or cotton. Both super-soft materials are hypoallergenic and inhibit bacteria, mold, and mildew. They're also easy to care for; just toss them in the washing machine and tumble dry. Also, buy a comforter one size larger than the bed. In my parents' bedroom, for example, I outfitted the queen-size bed with a king-size comforter. It's a small luxury that makes cold winter nights something to look forward to.

When choosing sheets, keep the temperature in mind. While there are lots of bedding options that promise "year-round comfort," I think it's worth the effort to use different materials for different seasons.

Keep colors and patterns simple. Look in your wardrobe for inspiration: Pick your favorite sweater, jacket, and T-shirt. What are the dominant colors?

Any bed can be brought back to life, despite its layer of avocado-green paint or dark-wood veneer, with a little sandpaper and paint.

In the spring: Choose organic cotton. Organic cotton is processed without harmful chemicals—when it's grown, harvested, and manufactured. Try an all-white bed: White sheets, white pillows, and a white all-cotton comforter without a duvet cover give your bed a weightless quality and provide your mind with a pure and simple environment in which to rest. In my New York City apartment, I added a bright orange buckwheat hull pillow for a spot of color on my all-white bed; the white sheets serve as a blank canvas and make the orange color "pop."

On hot summer nights: Nothing beats the durability and coolness of hemp. Hemp sheets over time provide the incomparable look and feel of vintage linen but in a long-life, easy-care fabric perfect for today's hectic world.

Two dining room chairs slipcovered with simple white canvas surround a mission-style wood table found at a nearby flea market. The table is only partially covered to let the beauty of the wood come through.

For cold winter nights: An assortment of luxurious bedding materials turns a bed into a sumptuous place to rest. Cover your bed with embroidered organic flannel sheets (I like using dark gray sheets in the winter; they remind me of my all-time favorite sweatshirt), an extra-large synthetic down comforter (with a hemp cover), and a blanket of recycled cashmere. Add a thick mattress pad made from cotton chenille.

A PLACE TO RELAX

Ask people what their favorite room is, and you begin to see an interesting pattern: Few people say the bedroom.

Insomnia experts say that the bedroom should be used for only one thing: sleep. If you use your bedroom for other things—like paying bills, watching TV, or chatting on the phone—you'll begin to see it as just another room in the house, not a place to escape to and relax.

It's easy to let the realities of life take over the bedroom. But for a really good night's sleep, it's crucial to create a sanctuary that is free of clutter and distraction.

What should the bedroom look like? Let's start with what it's not: It's not an extension of your office. It's not an at-home movie theater. A bedroom is what the name suggests, a room with a bed. Throw in a bedside table, a chair, and a few accessories, and you've got an oasis all your own. Cover the bed in comfortable all-white sheets, close your eyes, and sleep as if you've dozed off on a fluffy cloud.

Okay, sounds great, but you want color. Instead of mixing and matching busy patterns, try sticking with just one color. Also keep in mind that the color of your sheets can make you feel anxious, bored, calm, alert, or relaxed. It's called color psychology. According to the Interior Design Institute, colors trigger specific emotions; one color calms us while another may excite. Here are some good colors for bedding and walls:

Pale blue: Light blue reminds us of the sky and provides a relaxing sensation.

Green: Lighter shades of green conjure up images of a breezy spring day. Dark green brings peace of mind.

Yellow: Bright yellow is a bad choice; while it may seem cheery, it becomes oppressive, and you'll become tired of it. If you like yellow, choose a pale version; it won't have the same effect as a bolder shade.

On the bedside table, keep a short stack of books you've been meaning to read, a small alarm clock, a reading lamp (a 25-watt lightbulb provides enough illumination), and a glass of water atop a recycled flannel coaster. Keep a recycled cashmere or recycled fleece blanket at the foot of the bed just in case the evening gets chilly. Distractions like cell phones and tax returns should be kept far, far away—the car or the office are good places.

And don't overlook the floors. Add an area rug made from tough coir or sisal; the rough surface next to your bare feet will feel like a mini Shiatsu massage in the morning. Throw on a fluffy organic cotton bathrobe and wake up feeling refreshed and ready for whatever the day has to bring.

RECYCLING THE MATTRESS

What, can't I just throw that old mattress away? Before you sprain your back trying to haul that king-size mattress to the curb, call your local sanitation department. Chances are you already have a program in place just waiting to recycle your mattress.

RECYCLE

In pilot programs throughout the world, companies are managing hard-to-recycle wastes such as mattresses, box springs, couches, and recliners. One company, Refuse Processors of Hyannis, Massachu-setts, has developed a six-step process for recycling mattresses:

1. Mattresses are dismantled and separated by material.
2. Cotton padding is sterilized and baled.
3. Buttons are reused and sold back to mattress manufacturers.
4. Springs are baled and recycled as scrap metal.
5. Covers are sterilized and made into cloth rags.
6. Wood from box springs is ground up to make mulch.

For a nominal fee, most of these recyclers will pick up your dry and uncrushed mattress right from your home.

If you're creative at heart, you can recycle the mattress yourself. While this may sound more Mr. Science than Conscious Style, it can be a fun project to do on a rainy afternoon. Invite the kids for an impromptu science lesson and see for yourself the anatomy of a mattress.

Fortunately, recycling a mattress yourself no longer requires making clothing from the layers of material you'll uncover. (Your kid wants to look *cool*, not like a *fool*.) The cotton padding can be finely shredded (either by hand or with a garden chipper) and added to the compost bin. Underneath the layer of padding, most mat-tresses will have a layer of coconut fiber; add this to the garden. The material will suppress weeds and add nutrients to the soil. Finish your good deed of the day by collecting the metal springs; most scrap metal dealers will gladly accept them for recycling. The best part is that whatever you have left, you can throw away; it should fit in one trash bag.

REUSE

When buying a new mattress, ask if the store will recycle your old one. Sleep Country USA, for example, recycles mattresses to assist those in need. Through its extensive recycling efforts and charity network, Sleep Country cleans, recovers, reconditions, and rebuilds mattresses, which are distributed to those in need throughout the community. This ongoing program has put tens of thousands of mattresses back into the charity community every year.

If your mattress is still in good shape, you can also donate it to the local Salvation Army or Goodwill Industries. In my guest room, the twin-size mattresses have been used only a few times. Because I wanted to replace the two twin-size beds with one queen-size bed, I knew they were good candidates for donation; I boxed the mattresses in cardboard, delivered them to the local Goodwill store, and received a receipt for tax-deduction purposes.

TEN *NATURAL* WAYS TO A SOUND SLEEP

Any doctor will tell you that one of the most important things you can do for your health is to sleep. According to WebMD, an online health Web site, "During sleep, your body produces growth hormones that help speed up the absorption of nutrients and amino acid in your cells and aid the healing of tissues throughout your body. The hormone also stimulates your bone marrow, where your immune system cells are born."

We don't sleep enough. According to the National Sleep Foundation, only 35 percent of adults sleep the recommended eight hours or more per night during the average workweek. The problem is so bad that the *Wall Street Journal* reported that a "good night's sleep is a

CONSCIOUS STYLE PROFILE: COYUCHI

To anyone else, the idea might have sounded overly idealistic, too ambitious, or even naïve: Create a line of 100 percent organic cotton luxury sheets without the support of financial backers or retail channels, and let word of mouth build business.

But in 1991, Christine Nielson did just that and founded Coyuchi (which means "natural cotton" in Nahuatl, the language of the Aztecs), a wholesale manufacturer of organic bed and bath products.

But as other manufacturers before her tried to sell organic cotton bedding and failed, Christine knew she had to do something radically different: focus on the quality first. "The goal was to create a product that is simple, beautiful, soft, and well made and do it in a way with the least impact on the environment. People aren't going to pay for sheets if they are frumpy or unattractive—no matter how eco-friendly they might be," she explains. Coyuchi sheets are simply better; not just better eco-friendly sheets, but perhaps the best sheets you can buy. Period.

Coyuchi's line includes plush towels, bath mats, and robes and 230-thread-count sheets, pillowcases, and duvet covers. The products aren't inexpensive, but Coyuchi's die-hard customers don't seem to mind paying for good bedding. "The first-time buyer is committed to organic agriculture and buys it for their personal health and the environment. The repeat customer buys our sheets because they feel so great," says Nielson.

You won't find busy patterns or distracting color in the collection. Instead, the design philosophy is very much in line with the Conscious Style Serenity Bed: crisp white, khaki, and simple striped patterns. Sleeping on these sheets is a real treat, it's good for your health, and the simplicity helps bring calm and tranquillity to the bedroom. And you'll sleep better at night knowing where and how the sheets were made.

Coyuchi's cotton doesn't come from large commercial farms, but from small family farms all over the world. Because these farms are maintained

(continued)

by hand and not with powerful machinery and harsh chemicals, the highest quality cotton can be obtained. In the process, buying this cotton helps people earn a living. "We're not going to change the world, but we can help support local and economically sustainable agriculture production." In Turkey, for example, Coyuchi purchases cotton from eighteen farms, ranging in size from 10 to 250 acres. All the farmers are paid a premium price for the organic cotton. "The organic cotton also means the farmers are not subjected to pesticides, which is better for their health, their community, and the land they live on," Nielson explains. And when farmers have an economic incentive to be green, they'll continue to use sustainable methods far into the future.

Christine is religious about quality and environmental control, frequently making site visits where the cotton is grown and the products are manufactured. Coyuchi also follows the strict organic standards set forth by the International Federation of Organic Agriculture Movements. Cotton seeds first must not be genetically engineered, insects must be controlled by methods that simulate what happens in the natural environment, and no chemical fertilizer, herbicide, or pesticide of any kind can be used at any time.

But if not for the environment, people buy Coyuchi sheets because they are so soft and indulgent. When you open a package of conventional cotton sheets, the smell of dyes and chemical treatments can be overwhelming—the dyes make the sheets feel rubbery. Organic cotton sheets are free of harmful dyes or chemicals and have an ethereal texture that must be felt to be fully appreciated.

And Christine offers this Conscious Style tip for the ultimate in luxury: Wash the sheets in a mild detergent, and hang them up on a sunny day to dry. You'll end up with wrinkle-free sheets, and at night when you sleep, your senses will be engulfed with the sweet smell of a sunny spring day.

See for yourself at www.coyuchiorganic.com.

much sought-after commodity . . . the ultimate perk for the truly successful."

When was the last time a luxury item was free? Take advantage of all the benefits sleep has to offer. But if you have trouble sleeping, don't reach for pills or a nightcap of gin and tonic. Give these Conscious Style solutions a try to help you get those valuable *zzz*'s.

1. Do the basics. Pull the shades to block unwanted light, replace the alarm clock with one that doesn't light up, and adjust the thermostat to a comfortable temperature (60 to 65 degrees Fahrenheit or 16 to 18 degrees Celsius is recommended).

2. Aromatherapy. To help my father sleep better, I inserted a tiny sachet of lavender in each pillow. The delicate and subtle aroma has been known for years to help ease tension, calm nerves, and promote sleep.

3. Practice rituals. Take a warm bath, eat a snack, or listen to calming music every night. This will help you relax before bedtime.

4. Make white noise. No, this isn't Paula Abdul, but steady low sounds coming from the whir of a fan or air conditioner. White noise covers any unpleasant sounds.

5. Wear socks. According to the Psychiatric University Clinic in Basel, Switzerland, wearing socks will help you drift off faster. The body prepares for sleep by widening the blood vessels in the hands and feet to help radiate body heat away from the trunk; warming the feet and then removing the socks helps promote the dilation.

6. Don't nap. Study after study has recommended avoiding afternoon and evening naps.

7. Keep a pattern. Ever notice that your dog wakes up at the exact same time every day? Go to sleep and wake up at the same time every day. This will help normalize your sleep patterns.

8. Meditate. Put the day's worries behind you. Sit in a quiet, comfortable spot and slowly breathe in and out.

9. Avoid spicy foods. Meals seasoned with peppers, garlic, or chilies can cause heartburn and interfere with sleep. If you love spicy food, eat the five-alarm chili for lunch, not for dinner.

10. Carb up. A chemical in the brain called serotonin aids in sleep. Eating a high-carbohydrate snack, like toast or pasta salad, an hour before bedtime helps facilitate the creation of serotonin.

CHAPTER SIX

REFRESH

There must be quite a few things a hot bath won't cure, but I don't know many of them.

—SYLVIA PLATH, *THE BELL JAR*

Years ago, we used to turn our noses up at all-natural beauty products, those dusty bottles found in the back of health food stores. We all thought only Birkenstock-wearing, tofu-making fanatics would seek out cruelty-free cosmetics and wash their hair with foul-smelling shampoo made from tree bark. On top of that, these products were ridiculously expensive and didn't work.

How things change. Today, almost every cosmetics company in the world refuses to test on animals. It's easy to find a bottle of shampoo with "rain-forest extracts" at your local twenty-four hour pharmacy or even in your hotel bathroom. The word *botanicals* is screaming from every bottle of moisturizer, conditioner, and perfume. Beauty companies hear the message loud and clear: Being beautiful on the outside means being compassionate on the inside, too.

Bathrooms are also changing with the times. More of us view our bathrooms as places to refresh before the day begins or as at-home spas perfect for reenergizing after a long day at the office; we are discovering that these rooms can be places of relaxation. But even

LEFT: The medicine cabinet is full of ecologically sound products and containers. Old tinware, terra cotta, and even chipped barware keep everything organized. BELOW: Organic cotton towels now come in terry and waffle design patters.

a jar of hemp moisturizer sitting in the medicine cabinet can't make up for the havoc most bathrooms wreak on the earth: gallons of wasted water, beauty products with layers of silly packaging, toxic chemicals used to keep sinks and showers "scum free."

When my parents built their home in 1987, they used standard materials in all three bathrooms. Lights, just like those seen in the makeup room of TV talk shows, stretched across the tops of the mirrors. I never turned those lights on, preferring to bring in a lamp so the harsh overhead light wouldn't wound my sleepy eyes. Large laminate vanities swallowed the rooms, leaving little space for the kids to bring in cherished objects. Everything looked prefabricated.

I decided to renovate just one bathroom during the three-month project. I let my parents choose: The first-floor bathroom was selected "since guests will be able to see it," my mother explained. The smoky blue tile and dark red wallpaper didn't conjure up serenity; I could already imagine clear recycled glass tiles, a vintage stainless-steel medicine cabinet, and oversize ceramic sink with real nickel fixtures. The renovation would be a challenge, granted, but a good kind of challenge that would give me a lifetime's worth of knowledge.

THE FOUNDATION

The best designed bathrooms are the ones approached with a workhorse attitude. No color-coordinated towels, potpourri, or scented soaps only for "special occasions." A bathroom should be beautiful for its simple and utilitarian design, as if directly from the set of *Gattaca*.

Of all the rooms in my parents' house, the bathroom was the only room where nothing could be spared. My solution? Get rid of it all. With a sledgehammer and wheelbarrow, I tore through that room like a madman. Once I hauled the tile, mirrors, cabinets, sink, shower, toilet, and lighting away, I needed some inspiration for this war zone: an organic cotton white terry towel. It represented everything I wanted the bathroom to be: clean, simple, and essential.

FLOORS

Carpet, hardwood floors, and anything that needs to be glued to the baseboard doesn't belong here. After all, a bathroom is frigid in the morning and steaming hot right after your shower. The last things you need in the bathroom are moldy carpets or vinyl tiles peeling up. Stick with tile.

White ceramic tile is strong, easy to maintain, and a good choice when working on a budget. Stick with tiles free of embellishment. This is definitely the time when the rule "less is more" makes sense. If you want color tiles, follow the psychology of colors and stick with hues that don't excite or dull the senses. The Switzerland of colors includes pale blues, yellows, and greens.

Another option is glass. When you use glass tiles, the effect is evocative of a soft, serene surface; during the morning, the tile will reflect cool light that peeks through the window. In my bathroom, I installed recycled glass tile that I had custom-made by Sandhill Industries in Fairbanks, Alaska. While glass may seem like an improbable floor tile (thoughts of dropping that glass fishbowl in the fifth grade come to mind, right?), it's actually twice as strong as ceramic.

SINKS

There really isn't such a thing as an un-Conscious Style sink, unless the pedestal is wrapped in mink fur. But you do have a few considerations to think about.

First, don't install a cabinetlike vanity with drawers. This is a clutter magnet for piles of beauty supplies, magazines, and anything else that you can fit in there. Leave the dressers for the bedroom, and choose a freestanding sink. Your bathroom should be a restful place, free of distraction, stocked with the bare essentials.

Also consider buying used sinks. In New York City, Urban Archaeology rescues vintage sinks from the unlikeliest of places: old hotels, hospitals, and apartment buildings built in the earlier part of the century. At the store, there are rows of these sinks, all dusty and dirty. So why would you want one? It's like your grandfather says, "They don't make 'em like they used to." These vintage sinks are the real thing—heavy, charming, and full of veins that come only with age—and all they need is a little bit of elbow grease to polish them up. Invest in new real chrome or nickel plumbing and fixtures, and you'll see why so many people enjoy mixing the old with the new.

But my mother would have none of that. She wanted new. So I splurged and bought a ceramic sink with nickel legs and an extra large surface to hold soaps and a small vase of flowers. But don't be fooled by its good looks. It is watertight, bolted securely to two studs in the wall, and all the fixtures—including the plumbing—are made of rust-resistant nickel.

TOILETS

Unless you're staying at the Stardust in Las Vegas, the toilet should be white, free of any decorative touches or accessories, like fuzzy covers and gold-trimmed anything, and—this is important to our water-conscious ways—a low flow. It's actually the law in many communities that only low-flow toilets can be sold. Low flows are good for the planet, do the job, and save you money.

SHOWERS

Choosing a shower can be more creative than pushing a prefabricated fiberglass shower into that hole in the wall. An existing claw-foot bath can be surrounded on all sides with three hemp shower curtains, reconfigured to be a shower *and* a bath. Remove the glass doors on the old shower and hang a white, hotel-quality shower curtain in its place. Make the curtain watertight by punching several grommet holes on one end, screw hooks into the wall to match up to the holes, and then hook it into place. Now it won't accidentally open and let a mini-rainfall pour over your floors.

HOLY WATER!

Did you know that the average person uses up to 200 gallons of water per day? The bathroom, not surprisingly, is the biggest culprit.

As kids, we were told not to keep the faucet running when brushing our teeth, and we knew that bulky showerhead was of the low-flow variety. Now take it to the next level. Here, some foolproof tips for saving water that don't resort to taking a sponge bath with just a bucket of water.

Look for the leak. Letting water leak from a cracked faucet or rusty pipe is like turning on the air conditioner in the car and rolling down the windows. Verify that your home is free of leaks. Go outside and read your water meter. For the next two hours, don't turn on a single faucet, flush a toilet, or wash a load of laundry—don't use any water at all, and check the meter again. If the meter does not read exactly the same, there is a leak. Call a plumber and get it fixed; you'll not only be practicing Conscious Style, but you'll end up saving money by getting the problem fixed before a major catastrophe happens.

Replace the washer. The simplest repairs sometimes create the biggest results. If your sink is dripping water, visit the hardware store and replace the washer. Why, it's just a drop of water! Here's the amazing part: If your faucet is dripping at a rate of one drop per second, you're wasting 2,700 gallons per year. For less than a dollar, you can stop the waste and save lots of dough on your utilities bill.

The dam toilet. Believe it or not, most of us flush excess water down the toilet. For older toilets, take a plastic tub—a margarine container will do just fine—fill it with water and place it in the well of the toilet (the place where all the clean water sits). This will cut down on the amount of water needed for each flush.

Also check the toilet for leaks. Add food coloring to the tank. Return in thirty minutes. If the toilet is leaking, color will appear in the toilet bowl. Call a plumber to fix the problem.

Recycle water. When you're waiting for the water to get hot, fill up a watering can with the tepid water. Not only are you saving water that would otherwise just go down the drain, it's a good reminder to water that thirsty ficus before you head off to work.

This hook is made from a rhododendron branch, giving the bathroom a rustic look. The towel is made in France from unbleached cotton.

Bring your tropical plants into the bathroom once in a while; they'll drink up all that hot moisture in the air.

Wrap the pipes. On a cold winter day, you wouldn't wear a light jacket to stay warm, would you? Wrap your water pipes with insulation; the water will heat up quicker, which means you'll save water and get that hot shower even sooner.

ACCESSORIES

Let's face it: Most bathroom accessories suck unless they come from an expensive Madison Avenue boutique. Shopping for a soap dish, toothbrush holder, and glass containers can be maddening. Try this: Skip the home decorating stores and rummage through your house for handy accessories.

Terra-cotta pots. You know those little terra-cotta pots you've been meaning to grow herbs in? Take them out of the closet and fill them with Band-Aids and little bars of soap, or keep your toothbrush and toothpaste together in one.

Recycled aluminum. There's a reason why aluminum makes up so much of those giant 747 airplanes: It's lightweight, rust resistant, and strong. In the bathroom, I replaced the plastic toilet paper holder, towel rack, and toothbrush holder with sand-cast recycled aluminum pieces. Their simple design, free of any distracting patterns or colors, feels substantial and looks good in the bathroom. Plus, all the hot, steamy showers in the world won't cause them to discolor, spot, or stain.

Chipped glass. Keep cotton balls and Q-tips at hand, store little squeeze bottles of antibiotics and ointments together, or corral your ever-growing collection of lip balm—all in chipped glassware, like wineglasses and champagne flutes. Just don't use them to drink water; one morning, you'll forget to look where the chip is, and your lip will look like Rocky gave you the ol' one-two.

Restaurant condiment bottles. *Bang! Bang! Bang!* Gotta get that last drop of shampoo out of the bottle. Stop the madness. Go the restaurant supply store and pick up a few clear

BEFORE: photos of my parents' suburban home and yard before the Conscious Style renovation.

I found this solid wood table at a junk store for just a few dollars. It didn't need any repairs whatsoever. On top, an arrangement of freshly cut sedum from the garden will keep for several weeks.

The sofa was reupholstered in strong hemp fabric, the floors recovered in pure sisal, and the wooden trunk is made from sustainably harvested wood.

Just about anything can be tied to the ends of pull cords on window treatments. These pottery shards add interest and texture to the wall.

The pillow is filled with fluffy EcoSpun, a respun filler made from shredded plastic soda bottles.

There's no need to use ordinary gravel when growing plants. Here, colorful river rocks look attractive while supporting these live bamboo plants.

The footstool above is covered with 150-year-old antique French ticking, and the other is reupholstered with a material called Treetap, a wild latex collected in the Amazon rain forest.

Organic cotton sheets in soothing whites and blues add a calming dimension to the bedroom. Organic cotton isn't just good for the planet—its softness has to be touched to be believed. The floors in the master bedroom were replaced with honey-colored bamboo.

Touches of durable stainless steel update the kitchen without making it appear too clinical or sterile. The original vinyl floors were replaced with hardworking, sustainably harvested maple, which was prefinished to save time and money.

The dining room chairs were originally covered in bright orange velvet, but after I recovered them in Polish hemp, they took on a sophisticated, elegant appearance. The napkins on the table are simply bandannas purchased at a discount chain store.

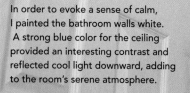

In order to evoke a sense of calm,
I painted the bathroom walls white.
A strong blue color for the ceiling
provided an interesting contrast and
reflected cool light downward, adding
to the room's serene atmosphere.

The floors in the bathroom were redone with
100 percent recycled glass tile made in Alaska.
Stronger than ceramic tile, the see-through tile
adds serenity to the bathroom and is very easy
to maintain.

Whoever said household cleaners need
to be hidden away under the kitchen
sink? Eco-friendly, homemade cleaners
look good on the counter, in attractive
glass jars and containers.

The bathroom underwent the most extensive transformation. Originally covered with maroon wallpaper and surrounded with gray cabinets, the bathroom now has an airy atmosphere. The ceiling is painted bright blue to add a surprise of color to an otherwise all-white bathroom.

You don't need to be an accomplished tailor to make a tablecloth. Here, fabric remnants from other projects are simply layered; I think the raw edges are charming. The chairs are made from 100 percent recycled aluminum and Environ, a recycled "bicomposite" material.

Peach, strawberry, and blackberry protein smoothies.

A handmade recycled glass bowl assimilates well with family heirloom pieces; a polished stone from the garden protects the tablecloth from stains.

Recycled glass has come a long way since its experimental days. Today, its clean lines and organic texture make recycled glass a handsome choice for day-to-day use on the table and in the kitchen.

An old dresser and mirror rescued from the garage were painted with white enamel paint and put to work on the deck. The large star was made by a local artist.

You never know when inspiration might strike. I placed this walnut desk in the kitchen. With some extra fabric, I covered an old chair and message board.

Sometimes Mother Nature provides the most beautiful artwork. Press an interesting leaf between several phone books, and preserve by clamping it between two pieces of single-pane glass. I bought the clips at an office supply store.

In the fall, I cut back the dying plants to prepare the garden for the long winter months. To protect sensitive plants, I cover the whole garden with straw.

Hose guards are an essential tool in the garden, preventing the weight of the garden hose from crushing plants. These metal guards are from 100 percent recycled aluminum.

Tickseed

In the garden, I used a piece of slate and a bamboo stick as plant markers. Tickseed is just one of many deer-resistant plants I grow.

squeeze bottles, yes, the kind you use to squirt ketchup and mustard on your veggie burger. Fill the bottles with liquid soap, shampoo, and conditioner (you can invert the old bottle on top of the new bottle and let gravity do its magic) and you'll have a cool way to store your soaps and shampoo.

A magnet. In most professional kitchens, chefs keep their knives nearby by sticking them on a magnetic strip on the wall. Keep your tweezers, a pair of scissors, a razor—anything that'll stick to a magnet—organized in this way. Purchase a magnet strip from the office supply store, use strong double-stick tape or putty, and adhere it to the inside of the medicine cabinet. Throw all your metal items against it and see what sticks.

SIMPLE BEAUTY: THE FIVE ESSENTIALS

The bathroom medicine cabinet is so improperly named: It's the last place you should store your medicine. Pharmacists recommend that aspirin, creams, and prescriptions be kept in a cool, dry place—not in the fluctuating hot, cold, steamy, frigid bathroom.

Great news! Now you've got more room to jam those face creams, hair gels, and perfumes you've been spying at the beauty counter. But wait: Don't fall for the beauty myth. Simplify. And a note to men: Don't skip this section. We bought over $1 billion worth of personal care products last year—*$1 billion*! We're all guilty—women *and* men—of buying more than our skin and hair really need.

Simplicity to the rescue. Here are the five basic things you need to look and feel great. And never buy products tested on animals.

1. Shampoo and conditioner. Wash the shine back into your hair with hemp beauty products. For dry hair after a day at the beach, nothing beats hemp shampoo and conditioner. The oil extracted from the hemp seed contains a substantial amount of essential fatty acids, which are believed to work wonders as moisturizers for your hair. You read that right: *fat that's good for you.* It won't get you high, but it'll cure that "baked" hair of yours.

Metal accessories always look good in the bathroom. These handcast, polished aluminum pieces are made by Azcast, a company that uses only recycled aluminum in its designs.

2. Soap. To be clean as a whistle, buy soap free of fragrances and dyes. Look for soaps that are also pH-balanced; even if the label says its 99.4 percent pure, that's marketing phooey and no indication of pH balance. And be a smart shopper: There's a big difference between unscented and fragrance-free. Unscented soaps usually have a chemical added that simply masks the fragrance.

3. Moisturizer. You don't have to be born with soft skin to have it. Protect your skin by using a moisturizer every morning. Look for a moisturizer that's oil-free, has at least SPF 15 sunscreen, and contains a hydroxy acid to help renew skin.

4. Toothpaste and toothbrush. All-natural toothpaste isn't anything new. One of the biggest sellers is Tom's of Maine. But a toothbrush? That little ol' brush? Does it really make a difference? Just calculate how many people there are in the world, and multiply it by the number of brushes an average person goes through annually. That's a big number.

   Biodegradable toothbrushes look just like plastic but are made from cellulose, a natural fiber collected from trees. Almost the standard in Europe, a good choice is Acca Kappa. And a tip from my dentist: If you catch a cold, toss your toothbrush away after you get better. It's a magnet for germs; you could infect yourself all over again with the old brush.

5. Pure plant essence. Cologne and perfume aren't good for the senses and for the chemically sensitive around you. Perfumes and colognes can cause those who are sensitive to chemicals to get nausea, muscle weakness, dizziness, and blurred vision. Toss out those overpriced bottles. Instead, dot your neck and arm with genuine plant and flower extracts. Do what my friends do: Dilute pure vanilla extract with some water, mix, and mist your body.

And a few Conscious Style secrets, finally revealed:

- Freezer burn. You've been up all night partying or trying to finish that manuscript, and your face looks and feels tired.

(I'm speaking from experience here.) Grab one or two bags of frozen peas from the freezer. Let them thaw on your face for a good minute. Puffiness goes away . . . skin tightens . . . face freshens up! Too bad it's only temporary, but it'll give you enough of a pick-me-up to look awake for the boss in the morning.

- Quit smoking. According to the author of *How to Wash Your Face*, a recent study showed that smokers who don't sunbathe show signs of aging in their skin more than nonsmokers who do fry in the sun. Can you imagine what chain smokers in Miami Beach will look like in ten years?

- Finished the morning walkathon for charity. Check. Took the dogs for a hike in the woods. Check. Brought the old furniture from upstairs to the garage for tomorrow's yard sale. Check. Your feet hurt, and they're dried and cracked. A simple cure: At the end of the day, soak your feet in warm water. Dry off. Massage olive oil into your feet, towel off the excess, and let nature treat your poor feet all night long.

- Disinfect your phone. Germs build up on your telephone, which can rub against your face and cause it to break out. Take a cotton ball, dip it in rubbing alcohol, and rub it on the phone to kill all those nasty germs.

- A good reason to adopt a pet: After a stressful day, go to sleep on your back and let your pooch or feline rest on your stomach. Breathe through your nose so your stomach slowly falls and rises. The weight of your pet helps relieve all the tension we build up there. A water bottle will also do the trick.

HEALING PLANTS

Why is it that anytime we cut ourselves or feel a cold coming on, we grab whatever is "maximum strength" from the medicine cabinet? Do we really need all those pharmaceutical medicines to heal a scratch or stop a sniffle? No. For the smaller ailments in life, consider all-natural, plant-based remedies.

SUNBURN

It's just like any other Saturday afternoon at the beach: You're sipping your water and reading a new book. Make that a really long book. Sunburn. Cut a piece of aloe from the aloe plant growing in your bathroom, let the gel ooze over the burned area, and say *ahhh* as it moisturizes and helps soothe that burned and cracked skin.

COLDS

A-choo! Pull out a bottle of echinacea from the health food store, put a few drops of the earthy liquid on your tongue, and say good-bye to sickness. Much research supports the validity of echinacea treatments, proving that it helps to bolster the immune system and fight the nasty cold and flu bugs.

Or go ahead and feed the cold with a head of garlic. Cancel plans for the evening (trust me, no one will want to be around you), cut the top off the head of garlic, wrap it in foil, and roast in the oven until the cloves become all brown and gushy. Sprinkle with cayenne pepper and spread thick layers of the sweet garlic puree on toast. The garlic and cayenne pepper give the cold a one-two punch by stimulating the production of white blood cells.

INSECT BITES

Call me "specist," but I like some insects better than others. The praying mantis, for example, looks up from the plant, cocks its head to the side to get a better look at you, and goes along its merry way. Get in the way of a mosquito or a bee, and you'll pay for it.

Unless you're allergic to bee stings, treatment is easy. First, yank the stinger out with your fingers or tweezers. Put an ice cube on top of the skin to stop the swelling, and add a paste of water and baking soda to help the pain.

Mosquito bites are a real nuisance—and a damn good excuse for a soak in the tub. Draw a warm bath, sprinkle with slow-cooking oats (not the quick kind, or you'll find yourself sitting in a tub of mush), and relax. The oatmeal will help relieve the itchiness. The warm water will ease your soul.

STUFFY NOSE

A simple cold is fine, but when your nose is stuffy and runny, you'll do anything to break free from the box of Kleenex. Buy a small bunch of eucalyptus from the florist, and hang it on the showerhead. Take a long, steaming hot shower and inhale the invigorating smell of eucalyptus. All that mucus will disappear. Now is not the time to be concerned about saving water; you've saved hundreds of gallons with the Conscious Style, anyway—treat yourself in your time of need.

STRESS

You knew it was going to be a bad day. You're stressed, it's the end of an eventful day, and—let's face it—Calgon isn't going to take you away. Fill the tub with hot water and add a few drops of lavender oil. Breathe in the sweet floral smell, close your eyes, and relax. Take a washcloth and let it soak in the hot water, massage in a few more drops of oil, and place it on your eyes. Relax. Towel yourself off and call it a night. Place a few lavender seed sachets inside your pillow and inhale the stress-relieving scent all night long.

HEADACHES

I'll admit it: For a pounding headache, I skip the natural potions and go straight for the hardcore, maximum-strength headache medicine. But for stress-related pain in the neck or a slight headache, try the Conscious Style SereniTea.

Bring some good, clean water to a boil. In a carafe, place crushed peppermint leaves and orange rind (save the orange), pour water over them, and let it steep for a few minutes. Pour the herbal liquid into your favorite mug, add some honey, and pour some fresh-squeezed orange juice in. Sit down, prop your feet up on the ottoman, turn off the TV and phone, and sip slowly.

CHAPTER SEVEN

WORKING @ HOME

The trouble in corporate America is that too many people with too much power live in a box (their home), then travel the same road every day to another box (their office).

—FAITH POPCORN, *THE POPCORN REPORT*

Depending on your point of view, the "work at home" movement in America can either represent the ultimate in luxury or a form of house arrest. The simple fact is that all of us, whether we work full-time or part-time at home, bring work home and most likely have an area in the home that we designate for work. It can be as elaborate as a separate room completely outfitted with the latest in techno gizmos or a seat at the kitchen table with our laptop and a stack of files.

A Conscious Style home office isn't put together with cheap-looking chairs, desks, and organizers made from plastics, or coated textiles and fake wood obtained from office supply supercenters. They're bad for the environment, bad for our health, and in bad taste. Anyway, who says a home office has to look like, well, an office? Instead, embrace the reality that more of us are now working out of our homes and need a place to get work done. The Conscious Style home office is the way you wished your real office looked: an antique pine table for a desk . . . a padded dining room chair covered in your favorite fabric . . . a pencil holder that, in a jam, could be a simple vase. In short, form and function. My philosophy

LEFT: Deep shelves on the side of this 1940s walnut desk keep the printer nearby but out of sight. The metal file holder was stretched and propped to keep magazines organized. **BELOW:** This trash can is made from laminated newspaper; it is sturdy and completely waterproof.

has always been that your home office shouldn't remind you of *work,* but should be a designated place free of distraction where great ideas come to life.

FURNITURE

When I lived in Washington, D.C., I designated a separate area right outside my galley kitchen for work. But before I sat down and started writing my very first book, I needed the right chair. Like Goldilocks, I wanted a chair that wasn't cushioned (too soft) or too hard. If anything, I needed a chair that was worn in, like a good pair of jeans. When I visited a nearby thrift shop to donate some used clothing, I found an all-walnut chair, probably once used at a teacher's desk in a public school, for a few dollars. It showed its age, with worn edges, rusty screws, and scuffed-up legs, but the construction was sturdy, and it was comfortable to sit on. When I paired up the chair with my stark metal desk, the modernity of the table and warmth of chair worked quite well.

Some of the best-looking, hardest-working furniture today is actually old: wood and metal furniture from the early 20th century, refurbished and refinished—simple, honest, and clean in its design. There's no need to buy new when beautiful built-to-last pieces from the past are classic enough to blend in with any decorating scheme.

DESKS

A desk is simply a steady flat surface. When selecting a desk, it isn't necessary to seek out only furniture built as a desk; any good table, whether it was a dining room table or restaurant work surface in its past life, can do the job. Make sure the table is at least 28 inches off the ground so it's ergonomically correct.

Sometimes even antique pieces were better designed to accommodate high-tech office electronic equipment. I purchased for my mother an all-oak desk from an antique store. Built in the early 20th century, the modest desk had built-in shelves on the side, originally designed to hold books. Today, those deep shelves keep the printer and fax machine nearby, saving valuable surface space.

Professional equipment can also do the job. In the kitchen, I replaced the old island with a long, restaurant-quality stainless-steel table. Smaller versions can be cut to size and used as a desk. Large vintage steel desks from the "Steel Age" originally sat in hospitals and factories, and can turn a small corner office into a chic workspace.

CHAIRS

Finding the right desk chair needn't be a difficult job. An extra dining room chair, draped with a simple white slipcover, transforms into something completely different. When company arrives, just remove the slipcover and carry it back to the dining room.

It's hard to beat the simple design of café and outdoor garden furniture when furnishing your office. Vintage pieces, with layers of paint cracking and peeling off, look good in the home, but can be uncomfortable. Soften the metal seats by adding a padded cushion covered in a complementary fabric. Resist the temptation to refinish the chairs; the chipped paint will look surprisingly nice at home alongside your modern equipment and furnishings.

Some of the best-looking, hardest-working furniture today is actually old: wood and metal furniture from the early 20th century—simple, honest, and clean in its design.

Old schoolhouse chairs, like my walnut desk chair, were designed for the contours of the body and were built with strong materials to withstand daily use by students. These old pieces, with colored metal legs painted in bright yellow or blue and honey-colored wood veneer seats and backs, can be found at flea markets for a few dollars. Their nostalgic appeal will work well in any home and, when creating a home office on a shoestring budget, they're a good buy.

STORAGE

Because my New York City apartment is my home and office, outfitting the limited space with all my office equipment was a challenge. To make the most of my space, I purchased a tall but compact vintage plant stand and placed my fax machine on top. It was a great solution to the problem: It took the fax machine off the ground (where I originally kept it), and the stand's lower shelves were deep enough to hold a stack of books.

An accordion-style metal organizer, made from recycled aluminum, was originally designed for use on the desk to hold files. When I stretched it by hand to several feet in length, the once wide slots narrowed to the perfect width for holding magazines and rolled-up newspapers.

Above the cabinets in the kitchen was just enough space for five wire gym baskets. The old metal baskets, once used in the locker room to store athletic equipment, hold important but not frequently used office documents and supplies. Also, by placing them on top, it extends the length of the kitchen, giving it a strong vertical rhythm.

LIKE THE PROS

Herman Miller, manufacturer of the cool Aeron office chair, revolutionized office furniture design. No longer were conference tables, chairs, and filing cabinets boring and flimsy. The company even made office cubicles look cool. But for every fly-by-night start-up, it's inevitable several will fail—ergo, lots of lightly used Herman Miller furniture up for sale. Dirt cheap.

Right outside Philadelphia, a giant warehouse is filled with used Herman Miller tables, desks, chairs, and filing cabinets. While lots of these look more appropriate for an office environment, there are good pieces to be found here: curvaceous metal table legs could be paired up with an antique door to make a desk, a metal filing cabinet could be powder-coated in an attractive color, and even retro all-wood conference table chairs could become cool dining room chairs.

You don't have to travel to Philadelphia to get the professional look for your home. In the phone book, look under "Office Equipment—Used" to find a local store near you selling previously owned desks, filing cabinets, and other office essentials. Remember, don't buy pieces solely for their looks. A fresh coat of paint at the

auto body shop can make the most utilitarian piece look surprisingly good.

Keeping your home in order is easy with the help of drafting cabinets and library filing cabinets. These wide, shallow drawers make the most of space and keep single layers of flatware, napkins, tablecloths, and cutlery in place and easy to find. Vintage posters, single sheets of wrapping paper, and even legal-size documents can be kept uncurled and flat. The possibilities are limitless.

Professional office electronic equipment can even find a place in your home. All the phones in my home were replaced with professional two-line speakerphones; their state-of-the-art look adapts well in any room of the house. Retailers of used office supplies also sell refurbished commercial fax machines and printers that perform like new and cost only a fraction of what new machines would cost.

CABINET VERSATILITY

What is my favorite piece of furniture? While most people would say an heirloom table or armoire means the most to them, I find the simple metal filing cabinet the most versatile and overlooked item of furniture.

A few years ago, I was rifling through my filing cabinet and noticed that some of the enamel paint had begun to chip. Underneath, I could see the stainless steel poking through. I decided to strip the cabinet of its paint.

Using a citrus-based stripper and a metal brush, I took away the surface and unveiled a beautiful, gleaming finish. It didn't look like a piece of office furniture but like a beautiful silver box that demanded to be showcased, not hidden underneath a desk.

NIGHTSTAND

In my New York City apartment, space is at a real premium. There was only one section of the bedroom that could accommodate my large mission bed, with very little room for a badly needed night table for my reading material and lamp. To fix this problem, I replaced my old nightstand with the silvery filing cabinet. The honest metal box, when paired with the substantial wood bed covered in layers of crisp, white hemp sheets, looked clean and modern.

ARMOIRE

Originally used in factories to store tools and supplies, large metal wardrobes were fireproof and built to withstand everyday wear and tear. These cabinets are still built today, and their timeless architectural design is perfect for today's homeowner who wants functionality and good looks. They're perfect for storing clothing or for keeping your TV, VCR, and other electronic goodies organized and together.

You can even purchase several rows of gym lockers from a junk store. A metal refinisher can strip the surface and leave the surface bare, or an auto-body shop can paint them with the color of your choice. Or, leave them as is. Store a row of them in the bathroom or hallway, and keep surplus towels, linens, toilet paper, and other household items at arm's reach. Hang paper tags on each locker to identify the contents.

BOOKCASE

In any large room, a good way to divide up the space visually is to run a row of tall bookcases down the center. But instead of placing poorly constructed veneer cabinets that will crack and break over time, use two or three metal vintage lawyer's or tanker bookcases. Mix family heirlooms, antiques like pottery, ceramics, and even a pile of rocks with your books to take away the clinical look of the cases, place a large overstuffed chair in front, and turn this new area into your new favorite place to curl up with a good book.

PANTRY

Originally used in doctors' offices and hospitals to store cotton balls, medicines, and bandages, vintage steel medicine cabinets are classic and fashionable. Given their popularity, vintage pieces from the early 20th century have become highly collectible and are expensive.

Fortunately, newer versions of these metal cabinets can still be found at hospitals, therefore creating a new market of used medicine cabinets that are only a few years old. When I wanted to buy a medicine cabinet for the kitchen to use as a pantry, I didn't visit a junkyard or spend my weekend scouring antique stores. Instead, I simply logged on to the Internet, typed *used medical equipment* into a search engine, and found numerous Web sites selling used medicine cabinets at a fraction of what a vintage piece would cost. These resellers aren't used to selling to homeowners—since they target doctors starting their own private practices—so the prices aren't inflated. The furniture is in good condition, needs little refinishing, often has doors covered in clear, shatterproof glass, and can be shipped directly to your home for a small fee.

KEEPING ORGANIZED

If you've ever taken the time to do a really good desk cleaning, you know what an ordeal it can be. Stacks of papers need to be sorted, filed, or shredded. Rubber bands are everywhere, pens have run their course, and a small fortune in spare change is uncovered. And even after you've cleaned up, it's only a matter of days (or for some, minutes) before the desk becomes a giant mess again.

An orderly desk doesn't just look nice, it keeps you productive, too. According to Accountemps, a national employment agency, executives waste about five weeks a year looking for misplaced files, addresses, reports, or memos. When you don't have to hunt for lost papers or missing office supplies, not only can you concentrate on your work in an efficient manner, but you also gain five weeks of your life back!

Tools that help you stay organized are essential to the workplace and home office. But a clutter-free surface doesn't mean replacing the chaos with unattractive plastic bins and organizers. Instead, honest materials like aluminum, tinware, wood, and even recycled plastic look handsome on your desk, serve their purpose, and turn the messiest person into the biggest neat freak.

RECYCLED ALUMINUM

The next time you recycle an aluminum soda can, you might be surprised to learn, it could return to you as a business card holder or pencil cup. A few years ago, recycled aluminum wasn't easy to find, available only from obscure catalogs or dusty out-of-the-way stores. Today, these simple organizers, made entirely from scrap aluminum that is melted down and made into shiny pencil cups and organizers, can be found at office supply stores, discount chains, and at fancy boutiques. All you've got to do is read: Flip the product over and look for the recycling symbol.

BATH AND BODY

Often, when we think of recycled plastic, we envision a hodgepodge of plastic bits, bonded together to form a confetti-like blob. A few years ago, when I had an excruciating layover at the Pittsburgh International Airport, I stopped by The Body Shop to pick up some soap. At the counter was a stack of tasteful tortoiseshell-colored cups made from recycled plastic. I bought all of them and placed them throughout my house: in my cupboard as everyday drinking cups, in the medicine cabinet to hold toiletries, and on my desk to hold pencils.

While it may seem odd to visit the cosmetics counter for office supplies, they are an excellent source for Conscious Style goods. At another store, a recycled aluminum soap dish, curved on the edges, was the perfect size for holding my business cards. I've even used a recycled plastic toothbrush holder to hold my paintbrushes; I simply slide the brush inside and place it in the freezer. The frozen brushes don't dry out and can be used immediately when I'm inspired enough to finish that painting.

TINWARE

A handy and decorative way to hold pencils, paper clips, and other office essentials is to store them in tinware. Tin has an extensive history, dating all the way back to the birth of Christ when pure tin was used as an alloy. Not until the early 18th century was tin used to plate iron and steel to form a utilitarian and beautiful metal known as tinware, a process still in place today.

Like vintage metal furniture stripped of its paint to show a warm gray patina, unadorned tinware has a clean, truthful, and even sensuous appeal. On my desk, I keep writing utensils and paper clips stored in tinware boxes.

Tinware, both new and vintage, can be stripped of its paint. Usually covered in layers of baked-on paint, the tinware can be stripped using some sandpaper and a citrus-based remover, and you can buff the tin with a piece of steel wool. To prevent rust, coat with an antirust lacquer and buff with any car wax to maintain the finish. Irregularity in the color of the metal—streaks and dark spots—are nothing to worry about; they only add to the charm of the pieces.

KITCHEN SUPPLIES

In Japan, restaurants often serve lunch in bento boxes, a compartmentalized container that holds a complete meal of rice, meat, and vegetables.

These beautiful lacquered wood boxes are excellent for storing small office supplies, like highlighters, rubber bands, and small stacks of Post-It notes. And since they're stackable, you can layer several bento boxes neatly on your desk. If you want something more modern, camping supply stores sell airtight, stainless-steel versions of the bento box.

Artists can benefit from Pyrex measuring cups. Those wide-mouthed measuring cups used to precisely measure out water and milk when cooking are deep and large enough (glass beakers will work, too) to hold a large collection of paintbrushes, crayons, and colored pencils. Look for vintage-style ones at flea markets or just pull one out from the kitchen cupboard.

TWIGS

One of my favorite ways to present proposals is to clip the papers together using a twig paper clip. With a small, flexible twig (one inch in length), use an X-Acto knife and cut three-quarters of the way down the length of the twig. Tie a piece of thin string around the uncut end to strengthen the clip. Insert papers.

THE PAPER TRAIL

Ever since I was a child, I've always been fascinated by paper. When I was thirteen years old, I searched all the nearby stores for a ream of recycled paper and was disappointed at the small selection available. Since then, I've collected unusual papers from around the world and use them in my presentations and proposals.

Did you know that the average person uses 68.8 pounds of paper every year? Of that amount, a small portion is recycled or tree-free. Recycled paper has come a long way since I was a teenager; today it comes in a variety of colors and textures and is made from an equally interesting and growing list of materials.

100 PERCENT POSTCONSUMER RECYCLED PAPER

One of the most environmentally friendly papers available, 100 percent postconsumer means only paper collected from residential and office recycling programs was used. One hundred percent postconsumer recycled paper is often identified by its substantial texture and earth tones; however, new technology has been able to produce 100 percent postconsumer bright white paper that is indistinguishable from virgin paper.

Be wary of "preconsumer recycled" paper. As the name suggests, preconsumer recycled paper is made from recaptured trimmings when conventional paper is made. While paper manufacturers have been using this for years, the term *preconsumer* was coined to give the impression that it is recycled. It's not—always look for post-consumer recycled paper.

BANANA

When bananas are harvested in Central and South America, the banana plant stalk is often dumped into the riverways. What would otherwise clog waterways has been given a second chance—paper makers are turning the stalks into pulp and manufacturing it into tough paper.

COFFEE

Every morning, I visit a bagel shop in my neighborhood and order the same thing: one large coffee with extra soy milk. I share the world's obsession with coffee. As it turns out, now you can buy coffee paper. The waste from the coffee manufacturing process is mixed with recycled postconsumer waste paper and transformed into a beautiful café-au-lait-colored paper.

STRAW

Animals eat it. Homes are protected and insulated by it. It protects your plants and prevents weeds. It's also an inexpensive paper. Wheat straw, an agricultural waste product, is pulped and manufactured into a honey-colored paper that is lightweight enough to replace the bright white paper found in fax machines, copiers, and printers.

HEMP

Producing 4.1 times more paper per acre than trees, hemp is a naturally acid-free paper material that has a shelf life of 1,500 years, ten times that of wood-based papers.

COTTON

You probably printed your resume on cotton paper. Used to make high-quality writing papers, cotton is a good tree-free choice when ordering engraved invitations, birth announcements, or personalized stationery. Use cotton paper sparingly; pesticides and herbicides are still used to grow the cotton, and organic cotton paper is hard to come by.

NEWSPRINT

Your boss says he'd use recycled paper if it weren't so gosh darn expensive. But 100 percent recycled newsprint is not only less expensive than regular paper, it performs just as well. Replace the photocopy paper with this off-gray paper and let your boss take the credit for saving money and the Earth.

KENAF

A member of the hibiscus family, the kenaf plant can grow twelve feet tall in just four to five months. Grown without the use of pesticides or fertilizers, and with very little water, kenaf converts to pulp easier than wood does. It also recycles easily with regular paper.

CARDBOARD

Recycled cardboard paper is considerable in weight and has a rich earthy texture perfect for letterheads, business cards, and postcards.

COMPUTE THIS

The last time you purchased a computer, did a faster, sleeker, better model hit the market just a few months later? So what? You probably don't need all those accessories to do what most people use their computers for: check e-mail, surf the Net, write a letter, balance the checkbook, and play games. If you want to save money and rescue a computer from the landfill, buy a refurbished system.

In the past, refurbished computers were the technological equivalent of a used car: You either got a real bargain or a lemon. Today, big-name companies like IBM sell refurbished computers complete with warranties and 30-day money-back guarantees.

The majority of used computers come from corporations that leased systems directly from the manufacturers. These "used" computers, most only a few months old, are fixed and updated by the manufacturer, and sold back at a fraction of the original selling price.

And if you're ready to replace your old computer, don't throw it away. If it's Internet ready, there are computer recycling charities that will gladly take your system. Your machine will be fixed and given to kids around the world to help bridge the digital divide between those who have access to technology and those who do not. (And remember to get a receipt for tax purposes.)

ENERGY STAR

When we think of appliances that eat up the most energy, most of us list the refrigerator or stove. But did you know that office equipment, computers in particular, is one of the fastest-growing sources of energy consumption in businesses and homes? According to the United States Environmental Protection Agency (EPA), office equipment—monitors, fax machines, printers—uses about 7 percent of all energy. Much of this energy is wasted, with an astounding 25 percent of machines left running at night and on weekends.

When purchasing office equipment, look for the Energy Star label on the product. "The Symbol of Energy Efficiency" will help you identify electronic equipment that meets the program's stringent standards for energy efficiency.

While many of us do not equate electricity with environmental woe, the production of energy to power our homes and run these machines has been linked to smog and global warming. The more energy efficient we can be, the less pollution we create.

Efficient machines also save you the other type of green: money. According to the EPA, powering a computer, monitor, printer, fax machine, and copier costs about $185 annually. If all those machines were Energy Star approved, the yearly cost would drop to $97.

The best thing you can do right now is to put your computer and fax machine on sleep mode. When you do not use them for a designated period of time, the computer and fax machine will automatically "sleep"; any movement—a keyboard stroke or an incoming fax—and the machine will quickly turn on and perform at full speed. The use of sleep mode will cut the machine's energy usage in half.

But know the difference between sleep mode and screen savers. Screen savers are not energy efficient; when a computer is displaying a screen saver, it is still running at full power. Disable any screen saver on your computer (contact your computer manufacturer if you need help) so you can realize the true energy savings from your equipment.

CHAPTER EIGHT

DECORATIVE ACCESSORIES

Beware of the man who won't be bothered with details.

—WILLIAM FEATHER

Have you ever wondered who has the time (not to mention the talent or tools) to etch two pieces of glass with a hard-to-find cream, solder them together with a special tool, wait twenty-four hours, and repeat the whole process the next day just to make a tea-light holder? The bigger question: Why does the tea light need a holder to begin with? Making decorative accessories doesn't have to be a pastime for the time-enriched. In fact, the Conscious Style approach to having a well-furnished room is to realize that the fewer knickknacks and collectibles you have, the better. Personal style comes from carefully selecting objects that best represent your individual taste, passions, and achievements, not undertaking labor-intensive crafts.

I think of decorative accents as multi-taskers and not "conversation pieces": A vintage cocktail shaker can mix drinks or it can hold a handful of interesting weeds pulled from the side of a highway. An old schoolhouse wall hook can hold keys, towels, or be used as drawer pulls. You can find an endless number of uses for a rock.

Presented here are some of my favorite Conscious Style ideas.

LEFT: A playful substitute for everyday candles, these candles and candleholders were all made using found materials. **BELOW:** I discovered this plate at an archeological site when I was thirteen years old. I use it to hold keys by the front door.

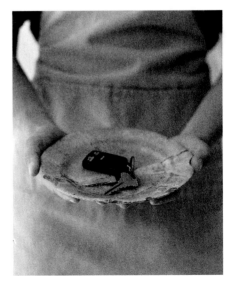

All eight of these projects can be completed in just minutes, and you don't need any special tools. These items do more than add charm to a room—they serve a function, too. And of course, they're all good to the planet because they use materials that you already own or can find in your own backyard.

FREE ART

I look at the great outdoors as the world's largest art gallery, full of amazing treasures and visual delights that excite the senses and inspire us. That's why I collect specimens from nature on my journeys around the world and bring them home to decorate my tables and grace my walls.

LEAVES

Pressed leaves are a throwback to childhood summer camp, where I collected interesting foliage from the forest, dried it between phone books, and glued it to paper. When you find an interesting leaf, press it just as you did as a child, between any set of heavy books. But instead of gluing the specimen to paper, center it between two oversize single panes of glass (which you can find precut at the hardware store), and clip the left and right sides with office bulldog clips. Lean the leaf display on a mantel or against a wall.

THE BEACH

A stroll along the beach can turn up the most interesting objects. Pieces of driftwood or branches from trees that have been tumbled smooth in the ocean can hang alone on the wall, be propped up on a table, or be used to support indoor plants. Larger, sturdy branches can be wired by an electrician and turned into lamps. Fix a wooden base for support and add a simple, monochromatic shade that won't detract from the natural beauty of the driftwood.

When entertaining, use a large shell with a wide opening as an ice scooper. To sterilize the shell, first wash it with running water. Mix a solution of equal parts water and bleach, and soak the shell overnight. The next day, scrub the shell with a toothbrush, rinse very well with water, and allow the shell to dry completely before using.

But be picky when beachcombing. When visiting a beach, don't remove natural vegetation or sand. Throughout the world, beaches are eroding at an alarming rate, partly because of global warming. The onslaught of increased greenhouse gases increases the frequency of tropical storms, which tear away at beaches. Another reason for the erosion is the increasing numbers of people who visit beaches each year, taking away sand as a souvenir (or inadvertently in our shoes) and pulling vegetation—like seagrass—which is vital for keeping sand in place. Instead, leave your footprints in the sand and leave the beach behind for others to enjoy.

HANGING FOUND ART

I don't hang posters or preframed artwork on my blank walls. Instead, I view my walls as an opportunity to surround myself with visual inspiration to motivate my writing and reinvigorate my creativity.

I hang original works of art—the older the better—to bring warmth and character to a room. But if you think artwork means original Picassos and Monets, think again. Oil paintings, watercolors, and original photography can be found almost anywhere, gathering dust in the back of stores, stacked on each other in the attic, carelessly tossed in the trash.

I find artwork everywhere. In my New York City apartment, my walls are adorned with original oil paintings by my mother, a framed botanical print I found in an antique book store, a very bad acrylic landscape I found at a flea market, and a vintage road map tacked to the wall.

A group of "found" objects looks handsome in the dining room. The framed photo was purchased from a local camera club.

Instead of relegating fine crystal and glassware to the china cabinet, pull them out and use them as intended. Mix textures and sizes to break up the uniformity of the pieces; here, heirloom Waterford crystal sits next to recycled glasses and a handmade clay pitcher.

PHOTOGRAPHS

A good place to start looking for photography is at your local camera club. These nonprofit groups hold juried photo exhibitions, awarding prizes for the best photos. Often, the organizations sell stacks of unclaimed gallery-quality photos to the public. In my hometown, I once found hundreds of color and black-and-white photos of Reading, Pennsylvania, in a junk store. Not only were they worthy of being framed, but they were only a few dollars each and had special meaning to me since they profiled unique aspects of my hometown.

BAD ART

Consider hanging bad art. A bad oil painting or paint-by-numbers acrylic may appear tacky in the store, but it could be charming in your home. I compare bad art to a shar-pei; with its layers of wrinkles and funny-shaped head, the dog is so unattractive that it actually looks quite enchanting. Bad art succeeds only when used intentionally: Devote a wall to a collection of bad art, lean a distorted oil painting on the nightstand, hang a poorly painted oversize watercolor in a sparsely decorated dining room. For some reason, it works.

YOU

Celebrate your achievements—and those of your loved ones. After my first book was published, I framed a bookstore poster promoting one of my book-signing events. For every book I write, I frame a single poster and build my collection. If you're an architect, frame a blueprint from your first design. Hang the winning baton from a relay race, the SOLD sign from your first home, a flag from the cruise you took around the world. Stray from the typical and look for unconventional representations of your accomplishments, and let these small touches of quirkiness fill your home. Another item I recently had framed was a funny article about myself in the tabloid the *National Enquirer*. It's so strange that I had to frame it and put it in my office.

A final word: Remember, like beauty, art is in the eye of the beholder. If you like it, keep it, and don't listen to what anyone else has to say. Rescue that dusty oil painting from the antique store, and frame that speeding ticket you got when you rushed to propose to your loved one. Hang these mementos up in your home with pride and let them give you a lifetime of inspiration.

RECYCLING CANDLES

As a child, I used to light candles and dip my finger in the hot wax to make a mold of my fingerprint. After I peeled the wax off my finger, I'd roll it up into a ball, drop it back into the candle's pool of molten wax, and watch it melt back into the candle. Perhaps this was my earliest lesson in recycling.

At home, you've probably got a small collection of candles that simply don't light because the wicks are long gone. Give these remnants a new life by making them into new candles.

Candles were among the earliest inventions of the ancient world, as shown by candlesticks from Egypt and Crete that date back to at least 3000 B.C. Making new candles from old candles hasn't changed since early Egyptian times. In fact, it's as simple as what I did as a child: Take cooled wax, melt it, pour it into a mold, and insert a wick.

The creative part comes when deciding what container to pour melted wax into. I like natural materials: dried coconut shell bowls, seashells, and the hollow inside of bamboo.

1. To recycle a candle, gather all your candles and sort them by color group: whites, greens, blues, and so forth. The colors do not need to match perfectly.

2. With a sharp knife, break the candles into smaller pieces; remove the wicks and throw them away.

3. Boil water in a medium saucepan, and make a double boiler with a Pyrex (or any heat-resistant glass) bowl. Place the chipped wax from one color group in the bowl, and let it melt slowly, making sure the water doesn't boil over into the wax.

4. Once the wax has melted, remove it from the heat.

5. Pour the wax into the natural container, wait for it to cool slightly (it'll form a thin skin on the surface), and insert a wick (available at any craft supply store).

6. Allow the wax to cool thoroughly at room temperature (do not refrigerate) before using.

You can also make your own candleholders. Vegetables, tin cans, and even plastic water bottles can be transformed into elegant candleholders. A pair of scissors or a sharp knife is all you need. Try these unconventional materials for yourself:

Vegetables. Cut an onion or potato in half. Scoop out enough flesh from one half so it's wide enough to firmly hold a candle. Flip one half of the vegetable so it lies flat on the table and the other half with the cut side facing up; insert toothpicks to secure.

Water bottles. In a pinch, clear plastic water bottles work great. Cut the bottle in half and lie the top half so the cap is facing up. Glue the bottom half of the bottle to the top and insert a large candle that will sit firmly in the container.

Tin cans. A fast and convenient way to bring candlelight to the table is to use tin cans. These cans, which once held soup, vegetables, and even Fido's dinner, simply need to be rinsed very well, have the lid and label removed, and be filled with sand to keep tea lights standing upright in the can. For a more dramatic effect, punch holes in the can in an interesting pattern to let small shoots of light shine through.

A TWIG LAMPSHADE

This project was inspired by Sally Wood, an artist in Napa Valley, California, who takes the pruned cuttings from her own Cabernet Sauvignon grapevines and recycles them into spectacular hand-woven works of art. The flexible and durable grapevine bends easily, without snapping or losing the outer bark covering, into handsome wreaths and baskets. In the backyard of my home, the forest was overgrown with wild grapevine. I decided to give an old lampshade a new life by transforming it into a twig lampshade.

To make a twig lampshade, find an old lampshade with metal ribs around the perimeter. Remove all the fabric, including any material wrapped around the base and top of the shade. Using three-foot lengths of wild grapevine (or any flexible vine), begin weaving the vine under and over the ribs of the shade as if you were weaving a basket. Begin at the base (the wider part) and work your way up. When you're finished, secure the shade to the harp of the lamp and tightly screw a finial at the top to secure the lampshade.

A lamp can be made from just about anything. With some wild grapevine collected from the backyard, I transformed an old wire lampshade (*left*) into something quirky and eye-catching. I was attracted to the shapes of a piece of pottery (*middle*) and milk can (*right*) and had them made into lamps; I was surprised by how inexpensive the project was.

ARRANGING FLOWERS

Did you know that something as beautiful and natural as a flower can also be harmful to the environment?

Most of us think that because flowers are plants, they must be eco-friendly. But even if a handful of carnations may be suitable for the compost after they've withered, that doesn't make them a part of Conscious Style.

ABOVE: A vase needn't be an expensive and cut-crystal antique. Here, an old track-and-field trophy, a beaker, and a pickle jar atop a candlestick elegantly display cuttings from the forest.

BELOW: I found this children's metal globe in a junk store several years ago. Its vintage look was appealing to me, and it adds just a touch of quirkiness to the room.

Most of the flowers at your florist aren't grown locally but at flower farms all over the world. They are flown into the country and trucked to wholesale markets. The sheer amount of gasoline needed to power these planes and trucks is tremendous. Also, since very few of these flowers are organic, a great deal of herbicide, pesticide, and insecticide is needed to keep those roses, lilies, and tulips looking their best.

Instead of arranging flowers that have more frequent-flier miles than you do, use what's in your own backyard. When the dogwood tree is in bloom, snip off a few branches, put them in a mason jar full of water, and place your "bouquet" on the table. Or grab a handful of dandelions or wild grasses and let them sit in your fanciest crystal vase; the wild appeal of the weeds when paired with the formal container reminds me of the movie *Out of Africa*.

Here are some other ways to display specimens from your backyard flower shop:

Trophies. Whether they're for perfect attendance or for track and field, old trophies are popping up at flea markets, swap meets, and even in your closet. Available in a wide variety of sizes, colors, and finishes, old trophies are great for displaying flowers on the dinner table. Place three small trophies down the length of the table with the largest one in the middle. If the trophy has a hole on the bottom, simply light a candle and drip wax into the hole to make it waterproof. Choose an unusual plant specimen—like a branch from a hydrangea bush or branch with pinecones on it—and insert just one stalk in each trophy.

Scientific chic. Those old beakers you used in chemistry class are also excellent containers for flowers. I began collecting old beakers a few years ago, and I purchased my first one at a junk store for a dollar. You can also find old beakers at antique shops, scientific supply stores, and even school rummage sales. Because they are often made from Pyrex, a durable glass material, they can be filled with water and placed on your finest linens with little chance of leakage.

Candleholders. Fancy candlesticks need not be reserved only for special events or even to hold candles: They can serve as mini-podiums to add height to an arrangement of flowers. Pick a glass jar from the recycling bin—a pickle or jelly jar works well—and place it on top of the candleholder. Use putty to secure the jar.

DECORATING WITH ARTIFACTS

When I was thirteen years old, I accidentally discovered a treasure trove of historical artifacts by tripping over a large crock in the ground during one of my walks in the woods.

After I picked myself off the ground, I pulled out hundreds of shards of pottery, glassware, and metalware. After having the pieces examined by a local historian, I learned my discoveries were early 19th-century artifacts.

While some of the larger, more impressive pieces were donated to a local historical society, the remaining pieces remained in my parents' basement for years. Instead of throwing the artifacts away, I found a decorative use for them.

A gray plate—crudely put together from dozens of shards with simple white glue—now sits in the family room holding car keys, change, and outgoing mail. Earthenware crocks, also glued together, sit on their sides like works of art in the dining room. With a hot glue gun, I even glued one or two tiny artifacts—small shards of pottery, a piece of weathered glass, a rusty hinge—to the front of a plain greeting card to add interest and dimension.

The next time you drop a crock or a cherished antique plate, don't throw it away. Crudely glue it back together and display it. The rough texture will add a new accent to the room. Old glass bottles, showing their age, look good on their own or holding flowers. Even a stack of mismatched antique plates—full of cracks and dark stains—can sit on a table by the front door holding your keys and a small stack of mail. And who knows? Maybe your next walk in the woods will unearth an archeological gold mine, too.

CHILDREN'S TOYS

I grew up during a turning point in children's toys. While most of my toys still needed the imagination of a ten-year-old boy to provide the sounds of cars roaring and army men plotting to overtake a nearby enemy camp, video games were being introduced to the market.

Today, video games are technological marvels that can dumb-found the smartest adult. But as those high-tech toys replace toys from a bygone era, loads of vintage toys are still boxed away in our attics or finding their way into neighborhood yard sales. Bring them out and give them a second life.

Vintage toys, when used in moderation, can add an unconventional touch to your home. In a junk store in Kutztown, Pennsylvania, I paid a few dollars for a toy globe that used to belong to a board game about geography. The toy globe sits on my desk, next to the laptop computer, printers, and fax machine. It succeeds at undercutting the seriousness of all the electronic equipment.

The key to using toys as decorative accessories is to not display them, but to use them in unconventional, utilitarian ways.

- When you entertain, throw a fun dinner party by having plastic army men hold up paper place cards on the dinner table.

- Old board games are the perfect material to make storage boxes out of. To make a square storage box, you need to cut from the board game five square pieces of equal size and one slightly larger piece (for the lid). If you want to make a bigger box, cut larger pieces from several board games. Glue the sides together using a glue gun or white craft glue to form a box. For the lid, cut two four-inch lengths of ribbon and glue the ends to the box and lid.

- Old children's books are often filled with engaging illustrations. Pick up several boxes of old children's books from a library rummage sale or used book store, and do what fashion designer Todd Oldham did for his SoHo, New York, boutique: Wallpaper the walls. Carefully remove the illustrations from the book (removing the binding first will make the process easier), and, using double-sided tape, arrange the illustrations on the walls in an interesting pattern. Pour white craft glue (buy a large container from a craft store), and mix it with some water to dilute it. With a paintbrush, wet the back of each illustration (be sure to remove the tape) and place it on the wall; when all the pages are glued to the wall, allow the "wallpaper" to dry completely. Brush another coat of the glue mixture on top of the illustrations to set the pages; the glue will create a shiny protective coating when it dries.

STONED

As Mother Nature reminds us, sometimes the best decorative accessories are free. Such as rocks. *Why not?* Collect large polished river rocks when you're out on a walk, or buy stunning specimens at the gardening supply store, and use them as spoon rests when you cook. When entertaining, place smaller rocks underneath the tips of chopsticks to keep your linens clean.

Tie unique-looking stones you find on the road or in your backyard to the ends of pull cords on your window treatments. The stones look more interesting than plastic or wood and they'll keep your blinds weighed down to let the warm sunlight pour in. Tie small rocks to any other pull cord—the ceiling fan, a lamp—to add visual interest throughout the entire house.

Stack flat rocks as bookends, place a few on top of piles of books, or keep a small pile on your desk to hold down papers and other lightweight things.

With a hot glue gun and handful of pebbles, turn boring bulletin board tacks into elegant pushpins. Be sure to clean the rocks first; any dirt or debris will make it difficult for the glue to adhere. Be sure to choose pebbles that are larger than the pinhead to camouflage it.

Keep your garden in order with unassuming plant identifiers: Take large slabs of flat rocks, and insert them in the garden near your favorite plants. Using white paint and an artist's brush, write the scientific or common name of the plant on the slab. And don't worry if some rocks are bigger than others—the irregularity is what makes the whole idea so charming.

CHAPTER NINE

OUTDOORS

I value my garden more for being full of blackbirds than of cherries, and very frankly give them fruit for their songs.

—JOSEPH ADDISON, *THE SPECTATOR*

Why aren't more people in love with deer, rabbits, and ground-hogs? Sure, they may nibble at your azaleas and feast on your lettuce patch, but is that grounds to proclaim war on them? Here's what I propose: Let's loosen our grip on having perfectly manicured gardens, become one with nature, and open our doors to let wild animals roam free through our yards and homes.

Okay, maybe not. After all, you still have these grand plans to re-create the gardens you saw on your last trip to England. And the idea of tearing up your lawn so a pile of decomposing logs can be home to some animals isn't all that appealing. How about a happy compromise: lush plants and flowers that will add beauty to your property and which our furry friends will leave alone.

In Green Hills, Pennsylvania, there's been a battle between the at-home gardener and resident wildlife for years. Hunting, which I consider banal and inhumane, hasn't done the trick; after centuries of hunting, there are more deer today than ever before. Deer-proof sprays and powders are the equivalent, I believe, of sprinkling Mrs.

LEFT: Under a lush, wild canopy of vines, a stone pathway leads to a set table in the middle of the forest. The vines have grown so tightly that the area is waterproof. BELOW: Sometimes I use a long extension cord to bring a lamp outdoors when I entertain.

Dash seasoning; I'm convinced it just makes the plants taste better. And all the fencing in the world can't keep a determined rabbit from finding a way in. The solution is obvious: Choose plants commonly ignored by visiting animals.

GARDEN OF EDEN (NOT EATIN')

When planning a garden, the first thing to keep in mind is that plants should look appropriate for your landscape—as if a gust of wind brought a seed to your property to germinate into a magnificent bush. Your landscaping should complement what Mother Nature has already created, not contradict it. A flawless lawn dotted with boxwoods cut into the shape of the Seven Dwarfs doesn't naturally accentuate the property, but rather makes it appear awkward and overly regimented.

Second, instead of plotting and planning ways to keep wildlife away from your azaleas, simply plant varieties that repel deer and rabbits. It's called compromising.

DEER-RESISTANT GARDENS

Creating a wildlife-resistant garden is easier than you might think. To get started, all it takes is a walk around your neighborhood. Which plants are thriving? What is being eaten down to the bare root? Bring a notebook with you, a camera, and take samples (with permission of course) of different shrubs, perennials, annuals, and bulbs. Get to know your neighbors, strike up a conversation, and swap advice. Also talk to fellow gardeners, local horticultural societies, and your landscaper. Once you see a pattern in people's suggestions, you can be assured those plants will be left alone by furry creatures.

The Internet is also a good place to compile a list. Type *deer-proof plants* or *deer-resistant flowers* into various search engines, and a myriad of sites come up. There are also online message boards that list ideas from fellow gardeners about the subject.

In my garden, I wanted easy-to-grow plants that could also be purchased at my local nursery. Harder-to-find varieties that I had to have, I purchased on the Internet; in a few days, live plants arrived at my door via FedEx. I also chose as many perennials as possible since, unlike annuals, they will return year after year. Some good deer-resistant plants are listed in the sidebar. Please check with your local nursery regarding suitable plants for your growing region. (Growing regions are determined by the average annual minimum temperature for that area of the country.)

Because some deer-resistant plants can be eaten by wildlife during their first weeks of growth (deer love the tender leaves), I planted the most bitter-tasting plants—chives and tickseed—along the border of the garden. That way, if a deer does nibble at a plant, it will be immediately repelled by the bitter taste and will avoid the rest of the garden altogether.

The extra work is worth it. One morning, as I hauled the hose to the garden, I noticed large hoof marks in the garden. The deer, inquisitive to see a small garden of Eden growing where a simple grass lawn once stood, came to visit. But not a leaf or flower was chewed or torn away. While the deer were curious about the new plant life, these unpalatable plants and vines didn't conjure up any grazing temptations.

CONTROLLED CHAOS

Another type of gardening is to grow weeds. We spend millions of dollars a year buying sprays, powders, and special tools to burn, poison, and rip apart dandelions, thistles, and native grasses. Instead of devoting a small fortune to getting rid of weeds, why not embrace them and grow a controlled chaos garden?

While it may seem like a contradiction in terms, allowing a portion of your property to go wild has its advantages. First, small animals, butterflies, and birds benefit from the pasturelike setting, in which they'll scavenge for food and burrow for shelter. Second, wild areas add another textural element to the property, the prairielike setting helping to offset the uniformly manicured lawn. Finally, maintaining wild areas couldn't be simpler: Weeds are naturally resistant to insects, thrive beautifully in any soil condition, and need little, if any, extra watering.

DEER-RESISTANT PLANTS

African daisy
Allium
Bellflower
Black-eyed susan
Bleeding heart
Chive
Clematis
Coneflower
Coral bells
Cupflower
Crocus
Daffodil
Daylily
Flowering tobacco
Forget-me-not
Geranium
Goldenrod
Hosta
Hydrangea
Impatiens
Iris
Japanese painted fern
Lamb's ear
Larkspur
Lavender
Lilac
Lily of the valley
Marigold
Morning glory
Perennial lupine
Periwinkle
Phlox
Poppies
Russian sage
Stonecrop
Sweet peas
Tickseed
Yarrow

There are different types of controlled chaos gardens. The first method is to designate a portion of the property to go wild—allowing "weeds" like wild grasses, goldenrod, and Queen Anne's lace to grow, seed, and reproduce. In other words, you let nature take its course. You can help speed up nature by digging up weeds from around your property and transplanting them. Also, in the fall when your weeds begin to seed, you can collect the seeds, store them for the winter in airtight containers, and plant them in the spring.

You can also have some fun with controlled chaos. If waist-high grasses already thrive in a section of your property, create paths that intertwine with the grasses. All you need is a lawn mower: Mow a curved line from one corner to the other side of the field. Doing so will create an inviting area that encourages people to walk through the grasses and explore.

The latest idea is to cultivate one species of a "weed" in separate patches. Prop stylist Michael DeJong grows a patch of wild thistle at his weekend house in Pennsylvania. The purple flowers, like most weeds, do not need any special soil or fertilizer to grow. DeJong simply dug up the thistle from along a highway and allowed it to grow and expand on its own. A simple edging, like brick or willow fencing, helps control the spread of the weeds while lending a sense of order to the wild thistle. If any weed variety grows too aggressively, pour undiluted vinegar at the base of the plant to eradicate it.

If space is scarce in your backyard, you can dig up weeds and grow them in terra-cotta pots. Choose plants with dramatic height or color; in a few weeks, the weeds will multiply and the pots will become a small collection of lush plant life. For dinner parties, bring the potted weeds inside and use them as unusual center-pieces.

HEALTHY SOIL

If you believe the phrase "You are what you eat," then it makes sense to give your plants a healthy medium in which to grow. Nutritious, airy soil will help your flowers produce more impressive blooms, allow young trees to take root quicker, and let other plants shoot out new, stronger leaves.

There are three steps to creating healthy soil: test it, till it, and add to it.

SOIL TESTING

Lots of master gardeners check the pH level of their soil on an annual basis. It is important to check the pH level to find out the amount of acidity or alkalinity of the soil when you are growing plants that need particular conditions. But when you plant easy-to-grow varieties or weeds, this step is unnecessary.

Take a visual test of your garden to determine the moisture and compaction levels. Testing for this is easy. In the location where you plan to garden, on a sunny day, remove any grass with a shovel. Roughly till the soil with a pitchfork or shovel. To test, pick up a handful of soil and squeeze it. If it stays in a ball, it is too wet. If the soil is powdery, the area may be too dry for a garden. If it crumbles freely, it should be about right. If the soil is wet or dry, adding organic material will solve the problem.

When I tested the soil in my backyard, the shovel wouldn't even make a dent in the ground—the earth was rock solid. The soil was mostly clay, and very compacted. To fix the problem, I transported topsoil from an old garden on the west side of the property, added compost and organic fertilizer, removed large rocks and debris, and used a tiller to mix and aerate the soil.

TILLING THE SOIL

Preparing soil is an important step to make your beds ready for new plants. You can till by hand, using a spade or shovel to turn the soil over. But an easier and less backbreaking method is to use a power rotary tiller.

In my garden, the soil was very compacted. I tried to turn the earth by hand, but the work was very difficult and time consuming. When I switched to a gas-powered tiller, the soil became light and malleable in a few minutes, and I was able to mix it thoroughly with the organic matter that I added. In just a few minutes, the tightly compacted clay became airy, rich soil.

When is the best time to till? If possible, till the soil in the fall, when organic matter—like grass clippings and leaves—can be mixed in and given time to decompose, which will add nutrients. Soil with large concentrations of clay benefit from a fall tilling, since freezing and thawing help break up the compacted soil. But if you plan to garden on a hillside, till in the spring. If you till in the fall, the soil will have no way to fend off any erosion from rain; instead, wait for the spring, and plant and mulch immediately after tilling to prevent erosion of topsoil.

ADDING NUTRIENTS

Because I am a vegetarian, I make it a point to add fertilizer to the garden that is not derived from animal sources, like fish or animal bone. While many commercial fertilizers will boast they are all-natural or organic—which technically may be true—it still contradicts my support for cruelty-free living.

Instead, I use an all-purpose fertilizer and liquid plant food derived from plant sources like seaweed and kelp meal. Be wary of fertilizers based on a variety of ocean matter; many of them include ingredients derived from fish. Because my neighbors raised goldfish, I used old water from their fish tank to provide fertilizing nutrients. The emulsion aids a plant's root development and overall vigor.

Compost is perhaps the best material you can add to soil. In general, compost is decomposed organic matter. A banana peel, some grass clippings, potato skins, and a bunch of leaves break down over time and become a crumbly brown matter your plants will eat up.

All you need for composting is a container—a commercial compost bin (look for ones made from recycled plastic) or something as simple as a metal trash can punched with drainage holes—and a few simple procedures.

To start a compost heap, simply pile up a large amount of "brown" material (leaves, pine needles) and wet it down with a hose. Begin to mix in "green" material—grass clippings, vegetable peels, weeds from the garden—and turn the pile frequently to let air circulate. At all times, the proportion of browns and greens should be about equal, and the mixture should be as moist as a wrung-out sponge.

When the mixture decomposes into crumbly brown matter, add it to the garden and mix it well with the soil. You can also make a compost tea: In a large bucket, mix equal parts water and compost. Let it sit for several hours (after the compost settles to the bottom) and use the liquid to water plants. It'll give a quick boost to sick houseplants and help transplants settle in their new environment.

Other good organic matter to add to the garden: decomposed leaves, used coffee grinds (for acid-loving plants like rhododendrons), and even sawdust. If you add large amounts of undecomposed leaves, straw, or sawdust, toss in some large handfuls of freshly cut grass clippings. There are high levels of nitrogen in grass clippings, which helps speed up the decomposition. Another good idea is to mow the yard and leave grass clippings on the lawn; they'll add nutrients to the soil and will eliminate the need to bag clippings.

Lots of gardeners also add peat moss, which is a practice that I discourage. Peat grows naturally in a living bog where plants grow on the surface. In these bogs, when plant material dies, it does not decompose as other plants do because the ground is saturated

> Deer-proof sprays and powders are the equivalent of sprinkling Mrs. Dash seasoning on your plants. I am convinced it just makes the plants taste better.

with water. Instead, it forms peat. These bogs, many thousands of years old, are home to rare dragonflies, butterflies, and birds.

To extract peat, the bog is drained, and the surface is stripped of vegetation, a process that kills the bog. All living plants and animals in the bog are killed and the ecosystem is destroyed forever.

Fortunately, there are alternatives to peat moss. Commercial potting mixtures now include peat alternatives—such as spent mushroom-growing medium, tea leaves, grains from beer breweries, and ground coir—and are easy to find.

TOOLS

Mother Nature never needed a single trowel or rake to create the world's lush rain forests or majestic redwood forests. But we mere mortals need a little bit of help. But do we really need five different shovels or a shed jammed with expensive tools?

Keep it simple. When I created the garden in my parents' backyard, I realized I needed only six tools.

Shovel. There are so many tasks a shovel can do: dig holes, scoop mulch, and—in a jam—bang a fence post into the ground. When buying a shovel, look for a stainless-steel one. It may cost a bit more, but the shovel will last you longer and will not rust if you take care of it.

A hand trowel (looks like a small shovel) will become your third hand in the garden. Perfect for a lifetime of digging in the garden, look for a trowel with a hardwood handle and a wide blade; avoid trowels with leather hanging straps.

Tiller. A hand tiller is invaluable in getting the soil ready for plantings. There's no need to buy a large, expensive tiller. Look for one that moves at least two hundred rotations per minute and is lightweight enough for you to handle.

If you don't want to purchase one, you might be able to rent one in your community. Gardening centers and some local and national hardware store chains will often rent out equipment for a nominal fee. That way, you don't have to commit to an expensive purchase and can still benefit from the convenience of using a hand tiller. Your landscaper or gardener can also come in annually and till for a small fee.

Wheelbarrow. Whether moving small bushes, yards of topsoil, or a bale of straw, a wheelbarrow can make an impossible job a cinch. Metal is always best (it's sturdier). Look for a wheelbarrow that can accommodate at least 400 pounds and has handles that are easy for you to grip and manage.

Clipper. Sure, you can prune trees and trim bushes with them, but you'll continue to find new uses for your clippers for years to come. I recently discovered that clippers are a great way to trim thick bamboo stakes to the size I need.

Keep the blades sharp by occasionally using a whetstone on the edges. You can buy a whetstone at a kitchen supply store. Also, sharpen your hand trowel and shovel to make digging holes easier.

Lawn mower. First, avoid a gas-powered lawn mower; they gobble up gasoline and emit fumes that are bad for the environment and your health. Electric lawn mowers are readily available, easy to recharge, and will save you the trouble of having to run to the gas station each time the lawn needs cutting.

And don't just mow grass with your lawn mower. In the fall, rake your leaves into a medium pile, run the lawn mower on top of it to chop up the leaves, and then add the shreds to the compost. This will speed up the composting process.

Garden hose. I've always believed that having a daily ritual helps to center a person in the face of all the turmoil in the world. Every morning, around five o'clock, I watered the garden using an old-fashioned garden hose. While there are numerous watering contraptions on the market that come with "smart timers" and space-age technology, I wouldn't trade my morning ritual for anything. Providing a drink to my plants as I watched the sun rise in the morning was my way of meditating.

I used a hose made from 100 percent recycled plastic (which

I found at my hardware store) and installed recycled aluminum hose guards throughout the garden to protect plants from being crushed by the weight of the hose.

Some other Conscious Style tips:

- Clean the soil off your tools after every use. There's certainly no need to sterilize your tools, but do remove chunks of soil with a wire brush.
- If your tools have wood handles, rub them with linseed oil and remove the excess oil with a cotton rag. This will help preserve the wood.
- Keep your tools dry. Dampness encourages rust, which is cancer to your garden implements. To prevent rust, fill a bucket with sand and vegetable oil (add enough so that the sand looks wet). After you've spent the day planting bulbs or clipping branches, dip your tools in the sand mixture.

GO PLANT A TREE

Every year, I try to plant at least one tree. Trees are shining examples of "givers." They:

- bear fruit and flowers;
- serve as a windbreak and can lower heating bills up to 30 percent;
- add up to 15 percent or more to the value of your property;
- provide habitats for wild birds and other wild animals;
- make shade, which cuts cooling costs 15 to 35 percent.

Before choosing a tree for your property, ask yourself a few questions:

1. Do you want a tree that grows fruit, nuts, or flowers? Or do you want a shade, evergreen, or ornamental tree?

2. What type of soil do you have? Is it wet, dry, loamy, rich, well drained, or a combination of these?
3. Will the tree have full sun, partial sun, or no sun at all?

After you answer these three questions, your local landscape center can help you choose a tree appropriate for your growing region.

PUTTING YOUR TREE IN THE GROUND

1. Remove all packing material surrounding the roots (do not plant with burlap or string on the root base), and soak the roots in water for several hours.
2. Dig a hole twice as wide as the root ball, and remove all grass surrounding the hole. (If you carefully remove the grass in large sections, you can use it to cover an outdoor table for an unusual tablecloth.)
3. Do not add fertilizer, peat moss, or any other organic material to the hole.
4. Stand the tree in the hole and plant it at the same depth it originally stood. Begin to fill in the hole with soil.
5. Finish filling the hole with soil, making sure that there are no air pockets. Pack the soil firmly, but not tightly, and finish it off by lightly tapping the soil on top with your heel.
6. Dig a shallow moat around the base of the tree, and water very well.
7. Add mulch around the perimeter of the tree, and water the tree thoroughly every week or so for several months.

FENCING

Flip through any garden catalog, and you'll see 10-, 12-, and 15-foot-high "invisible" fencing designed to stop deer and other wildlife from entering your garden. How unfortunate that you need to create a barricade from the world; instead of building a Great Wall, just don't build one at all.

If you plant a deer-resistant garden, you'll need minimal fencing.

In fact, the only reason you may want to fence in the garden is to keep Fido from digging up the plants. But a good reason to add edging, waist-high border fencing, and trellises to your property is to keep plants in order, provide support for vine plants, and add structural interest to the garden.

FROM LEFT TO RIGHT, a few Conscious Style edging ideas: Graceful galvanized wire keeps the lawn mower away but doesn't look obtrusive in the garden; curved rusty iron edging protects the base of the dogwood tree; a waist-high, free-forming fence made from willow (strengthened with wire) hides the compost and looks good, too.

First, avoid plastic fencing at all costs. At discount stores, you can find faux wood trellises and edging that are inexpensive. But they are flimsy, unattractive, and antithetical to a natural garden. Instead, invest in wood, stone, brick, or even uncoated metal materials for the garden. They look better, serve their purpose, and add (instead of subtract) aesthetic qualities to the garden.

In my garden, I used willow, bamboo, and stone to add geometrical and textural elements. Because this is a new garden, and plants haven't fully matured, it made sense to put willow fences around the four square gardens to add order and visual interest. The edging also prevented the lawn mower from accidentally cutting down small, immature plants.

I also added bamboo trellises—made simply by standing three long bamboo poles against each other and tying them together with jute to form a tepee—which added height to the garden and supported the honeysuckle, beans, and clematis vines.

I used tall, freestanding willow fencing to hide the compost bin. The upright willow branches, supported with galvanized wire for strength, worked well as a natural screen because they could be twisted to follow the shape of the compost bin. Instead of relegating the compost bin to a faraway location on the property, I can have it nearby without it being an eyesore.

You can also use trellises or any conical support device in the woods. In the backyard, I dotted the landscape with willow trellises. Wild vines grew onto the structures, adding a subtle artistic element that drew the eye to the beauty of the wilderness and its surrounding plants.

MULCH

One of the simplest and most beneficial practices you can do for your garden is to mulch. Mulch can either be organic—grass clippings, straw, bark chips—or inorganic—stone, plastic. Whenever possible, choose an organic mulch, since it can be incorporated into the soil after the growing season to add nutrients to the garden.

Using mulch in the garden

- protects the soil from erosion;
- reduces compaction from the impact of the elements;
- conserves moisture, reducing the need for frequent waterings;
- maintains a more even soil temperature;
- prevents weed growth.

When choosing mulch, avoid any made from tree sources. While some bark mulches are by-products of scrap wood, some come from trees that were specifically cut for the purposes of making mulch. Some good organic nontree mulches include:

Cocoa bean. A natural by-product of the cocoa plant, cocoa bean shells are an excellent and ecologically sound mulch. Unlike fresh bark mulch products, cocoa bean mulch is

Relaxing in my favorite outdoor spot.

lightweight, easy to spread, and improves the soil as it decomposes. Cocoa mulch is an excellent weed deterrent; watering it activates a natural gum, which binds the cocoa shells into a loosely knit porous mat that holds moisture in, but suppresses weed growth. Once the mat is formed, no amount of wind or rain will blow the shells away. But here's my favorite part: After a light afternoon rainstorm, the smell of chocolate permeates the air.

Straw. Straw is an excellent ground covering that helps prevent weeds from growing and adds a layer of protection for freshly planted shrubs and flowers. The yellowish color isn't a distraction in the garden, and this mulch is reminiscent of simple Colonial gardens. It's also an excellent choice for vegetable gardens, since it'll do its job and, at the end of the growing season, can easily be tilled into the garden to add nutrients to the soil.

Newspaper. Instead of spraying harmful chemicals on your garden to kill weeds (or if the thought of pulling hundreds of dandelions by hand makes you shudder), try a newspaper. Cover the ground with two or three sheets of newspaper, hold down the corners with rocks or bricks, and let science do its trick. The newspaper blocks out sunlight, and the weeds will eventually die. Don't worry about rain decomposing the newspaper; the newsprint will break down into the soil.

Grass clippings. One of the best things you can do for your yard is to mow the lawn and let grass clippings decompose back into it. But if you need mulch for the garden, collect grass clippings and spread a thick layer in the garden. Don't wait to use grass clippings—a mound of clippings quickly rots in the sun.

WILD ABOUT WILDLIFE

When I was twelve years old, I became a vegetarian because of my love for animals. Naturally, living in rural Pennsylvania, I grew quite fascinated with the wild animals that lived around our property.

While it may seem tempting to bring food to deer, game birds, and rabbits, numerous wildlife experts advise against it. According to Mike Markarian of the Fund for Animals, feeding wild animals "desensitizes them to human beings," and they become dependent on us for food. To make sure wild animals remain wild, the best thing you can do is nothing.

The best time to plant a tree is on a drizzly, overcast day.

But that doesn't mean you shouldn't help wildlife. Here are some Conscious Style tips to help you live in harmony with wild animals.

1. Cover your basement window wells with plastic protective guards. Small animals can easily fall into the wells and get trapped.
2. If wild animals rummage through your trash cans, use a bear-proof garbage can (available at any hardware store). The airtight garbage can will prevent wild animals from being attracted to the smell of food.
3. In the spring, review your yard for any rabbit nests. When you find a nest with baby rabbits, mark the area with a bamboo pole and do not mow the lawn on or around the nest.
4. Clean bird feeders frequently, at least four times a year. Birds can get sick from dirty feeders, so a solution of warm

water and soap (with a tiny bit of bleach to disinfect) will keep them sanitized. Be sure to rinse the feeder very well after washing.

5. Don't remove fallen trees in the forest. These decomposing trees are home to animals and are integral to the biodiversity of the forest.

6. Plant berry bushes for the animals. At my parents' house, I grew a patch of blackberry bushes; numerous birds eat the berries throughout the summer and fall.

OUTDOOR LIVING

Everyone loves to eat dinner under a starlit sky with friends. Having the discipline to actually do it is another thing.

You may have a neighbor who has added an elaborate wood gazebo or addition that's outfitted with every possible gadget and gizmo (we all do). But unless your name is Bob Vila, forget the wood gazebo; gazebos are expensive and often made from lumber taken from clear-cut forests. Instead, keep everything simple. At home, I stretched a brown tarp I found in the garage (punched with grommet holes for drainage) between four trees and created a waterproof canopy. Underneath, I placed two metal chairs that I found at a flea market and refinished with sage green enamel paint. This area has become a favorite of mine during light rainstorms; protected from the elements, I am soothed by the pitter-patter of the rain falling on the canopy. Sometimes, a parade of wildlife will quietly walk by, look up at me, and go on their way.

Deeper in the woods, wild vines created a lush canopy. I cleared a rough path to the canopy, made with slabs or rocks and granite remnants from a construction site, lightly raked away debris, and set up some old wooden chairs and a drop-leaf table. The area is perfect for entertaining; the canopy provides shade and protects from rain, and the environment is unusual enough to make the evening even more special. At night, I hang candle lanterns to bring subtle light to the area.

When buying outdoor furniture, plastic is not an option. Cheaply made chairs and tables may save you money in the short term, but in the long term, they will break, be uncomfortable, and be an eyesore. But buying attractive wood and metal furniture won't break the bank either. You can find well made, inexpensive furniture perfect for outdoor use. Some good options:

Refurbish. A year before the renovation, my mother purchased an outdoor metal table. But that was exactly the problem; it looked like *outdoor* furniture. I think outdoor furniture should easily assimilate with indoor furnishings. Instead of replacing the set, I had the white enamel paint sandblasted off the table to reveal the stainless-steel grain underneath. I mixed the refurbished table with a set of new office chairs made from recycled aluminum and Environ, a recycled bicomposite material.

Flea markets, vintage stores, and thrift shops are good places to find old metal furniture with a retro or Victorian design influence. I like both styles and have paired intricately designed chairs with spare modern tables. When you find metal furniture at secondhand stores, it may cost only a few dollars, but it's often in need of repair. Refurbishing metal furniture couldn't be easier: Lightly sandpaper the surface to remove rust and chipped paint, wash it with warm, soapy water, and apply a few layers of high-gloss enamel paint. It really is that simple.

Water hyacinth. Despite its lovely name, water hyacinth is an invasive plant species taking over the African shorelines of Lake Victoria. Introduced into ponds and lakes as an ornamental plant in the 1960s, water hyacinth today infests over 80 percent of Uganda's shoreline. The problem is so serious that the World Bank has set up a project known as the Lake Victoria Environmental Management Programme to control the plant.

Because there is no natural predator for water hyacinth, the plant species thrives too well, choking out native plant and animal life. And while it may seem ideal to use herbicides to kill the plant once and for all, the long-term effects to the waterways are still unknown.

One way to help is to purchase furniture made from dried water hyacinth sheaths. Local citizens are hired to collect the plant by hand, dry it in the hot sun, and weave it into rattanlike furniture. The soft, durable, honey-colored furniture—including chairs, ottomans, and chaise longues—can be used indoors or outdoors.

Wicker. When I was a kid, my mother purchased a set of bright blue wicker furniture for the porch. After all those years of rain, snow, and sun, the chairs didn't crack or splinter. Because of their classic good looks and durability, I decided to refurbish the chairs for the deck.

Using a high-gloss enamel paint, I painted the chairs light green and added unbleached cotton cushions. For the backs of the chairs, I covered synthetic down pillows in a classic green ticking fabric.

Good-quality wicker furniture can easily be found at flea markets and used furniture stores at nominal prices. Because these pieces are often painted in bright, unattractive colors, many people simply pass on by, not realizing the possibilities. But by refinishing wicker furniture with a paint that matches with an outdoor color palette—light gray to match the granite walkway, sage green from your favorite perennial, dark brown inspired by a tree's bark—you'll bring that hot pink love seat up to date in minutes.

Bamboo. In the colonial Far East, porches and garden rooms were filled with bamboo furniture for its beauty and durability. With graining comparable to the rarest exotic woods, bamboo isn't a tree, but a large grass variety with woody stems. Found in tropical regions, bamboo grows quickly, as much as one foot per day; it's one of the greenest materials you can purchase.

CHAPTER TEN

TAKING CARE

Neurotics build castles in the air, psychotics live in them.
My mother cleans them.

—RITA RUDNER

Of all the jobs we have to do, cleaning is surely one most of us wish to avoid. And yet, sinks get dirty, clothes need to be washed, and dust bunnies seem to reproduce at the speed of light. Without the help of a housekeeper, cleaning the home is a chore all of us must face. While we may feel safe using the cleaners, creams, and sprays that are antibacterial and industrial strength (and also instruct us to wear rubber gloves and use them in "well-ventilated rooms"), you might think twice after reading this.

According to the Consumer Product Safety Commission, the average American home contains 63 hazardous products that together contain hundreds of different chemicals. The Environmental Protection Agency has stated that the concentration of chemicals in most homes is two to five times higher than in outdoor air. Concentrations are high because cleaners (and body care products) release toxic fumes into the air, even through layers of plastic and paper packaging. One of the best things you can do to start leading a healthy life is to clear your home of these hazardous products.

The good news is that lots of nontoxic cleaning products are

LEFT: Clothing dries in the warm sun, taking on the sweet smells of the outdoors. BELOW: Beautiful and comfy organic cotton sheets.

available in the supermarket aisle. But by using a few common, inexpensive ingredients, it's possible to whip up your own cleansers right at home.

CLEANING UP

If the cabinet underneath your kitchen sink is overflowing with cleansers, it's time to simplify: Make your own cleaning solutions. But don't think this is a time-consuming process. What if I told you that making Conscious Style cleansers is so easy you can do it in just minutes with easy-to-find ingredients and save money, too? Finally, it's possible.

A quick trip to the supermarket leads you to all the ingredients you need to keep your home spotless. Simple, all-natural products like baking soda, salt, and lemon juice are the basis of hardworking, practical cleaners. Grandma knows best—these homespun ideas really do work.

CLEANING CLOTHES

We all want clean, fresh-smelling clothing. But did you know that conventional detergents are usually tested on animals and cause havoc on our waterways? The phosphate levels in most detergents cause rivers and lake to produce an overabundance of aquatic plants, which literally chokes out all the wildlife. Fortunately, there are lots of good brand-name phosphate-free detergents available; you can buy them at most natural food stores or online. (See the "Resource Guide," beginning on page 153.) You can also make your own laundry detergent.

CONSCIOUS STYLE ALL-PURPOSE DETERGENT
    4 cups soap flakes
    2 cups washing soda
    2 cups borax (a colorless, crystalline salt commonly
      found at the drugstore)

Mix together a giant batch of homemade detergent, store it in a wide-mouth glass storage jar (use a stainless-steel measuring cup as a scoop), and use it as you would any detergent.

LAUNDRY STAIN REMOVER

1 cup ammonia

1 cup white vinegar

½ cup baking soda

4 tablespoons liquid soap

SOME ESSENTIAL OILS TO CONSIDER:

TO ALLEVIATE:	USE:
Anger	Chamomile
Anxiety	Cedarwood
Lack of Concentration	Eucalyptus
Mental Exhaustion	Frankincense
Hyperactivity	Clary Sage, Lavender
Insomnia	Chamomile, Clary Sage, Lavender, Tangerine, Ylang-Ylang
Stress	Geranium, Juniper, Marjoram
Worry	Chamomile

Here's a great way to get out really, really tough stains. Mix all the ingredients above and store the solution in a hard plastic spray bottle. Apply the mixture to the stain, allow it to saturate the fabric for a few minutes, and wash with your other laundry.

Aromatherapy has been used for thousands of years all over the world. Ancient Egyptians used essential oils in cosmetics and in embalming. Today, people use aromatherapy to help improve the quality of life and relieve health problems. With a drop of essential oil, you can add a subtle scent to your clothes when ironing them. Add a drop or two of pure peppermint oil to a small spray bottle filled with water. Mist clothing before ironing and breathe in the invigorating scent.

BRIGHTENING CLOTHES

Did you know that chlorine bleach, which is often touted to be "as safe as salt" on the bottle, can be dangerous to your health and the environment? According to Friends of the Earth, waste chlorine bleach is flushed into the sewer system (or septic tank), where it reacts with organic materials to create poisonous compounds called trihalomethanes (THMs). THMs have been linked to cancer and birth defects.

There are many alternatives to chlorine bleach that brighten clothes and are safe for the environment. The simple solution here is to buy bleach made with hydrogen peroxide, not chlorine. As an added benefit, most of these brands are tested for safety without the use of animals.

Another simple way to brighten fabrics is to use ammonia. Just add ½ cup of white ammonia to the rinse cycle, and your clothes should look just as good as the day you bought them.

DRYING

When using the dryer, dry several loads of laundry one right after another. This is a great way to save energy. The warm heat from the first batch of clothing will speed up the drying time for the next load.

Some of the nicest things in life are free. On a warm, sunny day, hang your laundry outside on a clothesline. I like to mow the lawn right before I hang laundry; the sheets take on the smell of freshly cut grass.

GETTING HORIZONTAL

It's hard to fall in love with a washing machine. But that's exactly what happened to me. I purchased a horizontal-axis washing machine (HWM)—it has a door on the front instead of on top—and it has changed the way I look at laundry.

An HWM preserves clothes, saves money, saves water, and—best of all—saves me space in my small New York City apartment.

Although these claims may sound extravagant, they are all true—and they represent only a few features of an HWM. If you're doubtful, I understand. Before I purchased one, I was skeptical, too. After all, how can a machine do so much? Today, all I can say is *buy one*. It will be one of the most environmentally friendly purchases you'll make, and a great investment in your clothes and wallet.

SAVE MONEY. Based on the typical cost of doing laundry (water, energy, detergent), an average American family will save $60 a year or more by using an HWM. In just a few years, the added cost of the machine (as compared to traditional washing machines) will have paid for itself. And by choosing a high-speed spin feature for your machine, your clothes will take much less time to dry. That saves more money.

SAVE SPACE. In New York City, space is at a real premium. Because an HWM has doors on the front, not on top, I was able to install the washer and dryer under the kitchen counter.

SAVE WATER. How a washing machine uses water is key to clean clothes. An HWM uses "tumble action washing" instead of acting like a washtub. The tumbling action pulls dirt out of clothes.

SAVE YOUR CLOTHING. Because an HWM uses tumble action, and not an agitator, clothing does not wear out as fast. Also, the spin cycles in HWMs leave behind much less residual detergent, which over time can irritate skin and break down fibers. There is a reason these machines are found at Laundromats and in the wardrobe rooms of major movie studios: They simply clean better.

SAVE EVEN MORE MONEY. Some local communities and states offer tax credits when consumers purchase HWMs. Ask your Department of Energy to see if you qualify.

CLEANING HOME

With just a few inexpensive ingredients, your windows will be streak free, your wood furniture will glow, and your antique silver flatware will shine. These Conscious Style solutions are simple, practical, and will keep your home and precious belongings as clean as can be.

ALL-PURPOSE CLEANER

    2 cups of warm water

    ¼ cup baking soda

    ¼ cup ammonia

This mixture can serve a multitude of tasks. Combine all the ingredients in a glass bowl until they are well mixed, and pour into a spray bottle. The All-Purpose Cleaner is great for handling the everyday smudges, grime, and dirt life brings us, but because it's made from such simple, nontoxic ingredients, it isn't a disinfectant.

DISINFECTANT

   1 cup commercial laundry detergent (see also
     recipe on page 136)
   4 cups warm water
   1¼ cups pine oil (found at the hardware store)

This homemade disinfectant should be used sparingly; it's safer than store-bought disinfectants, but isn't 100 percent biodegradable. Use it once a month to kill bacteria and other microbial contaminants. (The All-Purpose Cleaner can be used every day.)

Mix all the ingredients together until the detergent is completely dissolved. Pour into a spray bottle.

A CLEAN SPONGE

When cleaning up spills with a sponge, make sure to disinfect it regularly . Under warm water, rinse the sponge and wring it out several times. Pop it in the microwave for a minute, and all traces of salmonella and *E. coli* should be killed.

Also, instead of buying regular sponges, which are made with polyurethane and won't biodegrade in the landfill, purchase sponges made from tree cellulose. They are just as thick and absorbent as regular sponges (in fact, they even look alike), but they'll help keep your home and the planet cleaner.

FURNITURE POLISH

Did you know that your salad dressing can help keep your wood furniture looking pristine and new? Mix 1 cup of olive oil with ½ cup of lemon juice. Whisk until the mixture is emulsified (when the oil and juice no longer separate). Pour the emulsion into a reusable oil spray bottle (found at gourmet food stores; it uses air to create a fine mist), spray the furniture surface, and wipe clean with a soft cloth.

GLASS CLEANER

Do you think that blue window cleaners work better simply because they're blue? Don't be fooled; it's just dye. Mix 3 cups of water, 1 cup of ammonia and ¾ cup of white vinegar into a spray bottle. Your windows will look spotless. And if you still like the ocean blue color, add a few drops of blue food dye.

WATER SPOTS

Why didn't they use a coaster? Water spots from last night's cocktail party or the kids' impromptu water pistol fight can be easily removed without the help of wood stains or professional refinishing. Dab a little of your toothpaste on the mark and gently rub with an old toothbrush. Buff with a soft towel.

SMELLY GARBAGE DISPOSAL

If your garbage disposal smells like, well, garbage, here's a great idea: Pour ice and lemon wedges into the disposal and turn it on. The lemons help remove odors, and the ice sharpens the blades. How easy is that?

CLOGGED DRAINS

In science class, we learned about chemical reactions when the teacher poured vinegar into a beaker full of baking soda. That same foaming action can help slow-moving drains unclog.

Using a funnel, pour a generous amount of baking soda down the drain. Add a bottle of vinegar and then a kettle of boiling water. It should do the trick.

CLEANING COPPER

Pour salt onto the metal's surface. Cut a lemon in half and rub the cut side into the salt. Tarnish disappears before your eyes.

POLISHING SILVER

Some of the simplest solutions work best. Instead of dealing with messy, caustic silver polish creams, you can just magnetize the tarnish away. Lay a sheet of aluminum foil on the bottom of a shallow basin. Sprinkle the aluminum with a generous amount of salt. Fill the basin with very hot water (it does not need to be boiling). Place your silver pieces on top of the foil and—*voilà!*—the tarnish disappears. (To prevent tarnish, add a piece of chalk to the box holding your silver utensils; it'll absorb excess moisture, which causes tarnish.)

PREVENTION

In an episode of the animated series *The Simpsons,* the foundation of the Simpsons' home cracks and causes the home to tilt just like the Leaning Tower of Pisa. Homer Simpson, after hilarious failed attempts to fix it himself, caves in and hires a contractor. After Homer spends thousands of dollars to solve the problem, the contractor says a simple twenty-five-cent washer would have prevented the problem. *D'oh!*

A little bit of preventive maintenance can have a profound impact on the life of a home. Not only is prevention economical, but it's a wise Conscious Style choice that can spare large appliances and other materials from the landfill.

Done right, which is to say simply and easily, these tips will help prevent a fridge, washing machine, or roof from having to be prematurely replaced.

1. Keep gutters and downspouts working hard to protect your house from moisture damage. Clean leaves, sticks, and pine needles from gutters. Scoop up the debris with a gloved hand and add it to your compost pile. Also, if you need to replace the gutter, choose steel over aluminum or vinyl. Aluminum expands when the weather gets hot or cold, causing nails and screws to contract. Vinyl gutters only come in 10-foot lengths, which means they have lots of seams that could leak.

2. Periodically drain several gallons of water from your water heater. This removes sediment from the bottom of the tank, helps increase heating efficiency, and prolongs the life of the tank.

3. Do not pour cooking oil down the drain. Liquid fats solidify quickly and create clogs.

4. Empty the lint trap from the dryer. The soft material can ignite and cause a fire, and a dirty lint filter restricts airflow.

5. Freshen the washing machine. Pour a large bottle of white vinegar in the washing machine and let it run through a regular cycle (without clothes). This will dissolve all soap residues.

6. Fix leaky faucets immediately. Leaky sinks and toilets waste up to 20 gallons of water a day and can ruin your pipes. Make it a top priority to have the problem fixed ASAP.

7. Vacuum the refrigerator. Under your refrigerator and freezer is a set of coils and a cooling fan, which need cleaning once a year. Unplug the refrigerator and use your vacuum cleaner to remove any lint, pet hair, and dust from the coils. Also, make sure there are at least three inches of air space between the back of the fridge and the wall to allow for air circulation; be sure to locate the fridge away from any heat sources, too (like a stove), for better efficiency.

8. Fix cracks. Use caulk to seal spaces where pipes or wires enter the house, around the windows, and where the masonry meets siding. Caulk can help keep out dirt, moisture, sound, and radon gas, and improve the general appearance of your home.

9. Freshen carpets. Sprinkle baking soda on your carpets and let it sit overnight. The next day, vacuum. The baking soda is a natural deodorizer.

10. Check the roof. Your roof takes a beating from the elements. Climb up on a ladder and look at the overall condition of the roof. If the shingles have separated more than

the width of your thumb, contact a roofer to have the roof professionally inspected.

It's easy to overlook lights in our home. They don't seem as important as recycling or installing a low-flow showerhead. But lights are important to a room; they set the mood and direct the eye to various elements. Some lights are even on twenty-four hours a day. Given our dependence on lighting, it's worthwhile to consider energy-efficient lighting.

If you're new to energy-efficient lighting—and really, who isn't?—relax. It's no mystery. It's an intuitive process like any other, one that sensible people can easily understand. Open a curtain, change a lightbulb, replace a lampshade. It's all that simple.

First, how many lights do you need in a room? Roughly, you'll need one lamp for every 50 square feet of space. For a room measuring 25 by 10 feet, you'll need five lamps. Of course, this rule will vary from room to room depending on usage, lamp type, and ceiling height.

- Let in natural light. Daylight is free, pleasant, and can brighten up a room. When my father asked how we could bring light to the family room, he expected me to draw up a complex lighting plan. Instead, I walked over to the windows, which had been covered with venetian blinds and dark fabric curtains, and tore them down. A flood of daylight poured in.

- Use compact fluorescent bulbs. It's obvious to me most people don't use energy-efficient bulbs because they cost a lot more than regular lightbulbs. We're savvy consumers, and when we see a scam, we avoid it. But the truth is, these bulbs really do work, and after their first use, they save you money. Those strange-shaped energy-efficient bulbs use 80 percent less energy, last 10,000 hours (which is ten times longer than a regular bulb), and, depending on the manufacturer, are recyclable.

- Be specific. Different lighting fixtures are designed for different tasks. Don't direct lights to the ceiling or floor. Choose fixtures that light specific areas, like desks and seating areas, for optimum effect.

- Change the shade. Light-colored lampshades reflect light better. A lampshade with a metallic surface on the inside—like aluminum leaf—will also intensify the light. You can buy aluminum leaf at any craft supply store; with a little bit of glue and a soft brush, you can add it to any shade yourself. Also, different shapes will reflect the light differently. So bring a lamp to the lamp store, test various lampshades, and pick the one that fulfills your need.

- Don't overlight. There's no reason to make each room as bright as day. Sometimes all you need is a lamp with a 15-watt lightbulb to find your way around. Softer lights calm the senses. Use low-watt bulbs in less frequented rooms, like the hallway and pantry.

According to britannica.com, lighting fixtures, as contemporary as they seem, are among mankind's oldest inventions. The lamp

I've always had a fondness for animals. But because of my hectic schedule, I know I can't bring an animal into my life. Instead, I often "dog-sit" for my friends so I can spend some quality time with the animal kingdom.

was invented at least as early as 70,000 B.C. Originally it consisted of a hollowed-out rock filled with moss or some other absorbent material that was soaked with animal fat and ignited.

Lamps have sure come a long way. They do more than bring light to a room: They serve as decorative accent pieces. And you don't need to buy them from a store; you can take an old wood column or vase and transform it into a lamp. I found a handmade vase glazed in warm earthen colors at a flea market and, with the help of a local lighting store, I transformed it into a lamp. I'm not comfortable with the idea of wiring a lamp myself, so I decided to save time and stress and have it professionally done. It's not expensive, and I ended up with great results: Its organic shape complemented the white dresser and light-colored wicker furniture.

Rewiring a found object and making it into a lamp brings old-fashioned charm to a "new" appliance. Search for unique items at flea markets, junk shops, and antique stores. The base should lie flat and sturdy against the table and have a hole on the bottom and top through which to run wiring. Look under *lighting fixtures* in the yellow pages for a local dealer who can wire it for you. Match the new lamp with a lampshade—preferably made from a natural material like burlap or canvas—screw in an energy-efficient bulb, flip the switch, and spend the evening with a good book.

CARING FOR PETS

Man's best friend is our liaison to the wild kingdom. Dogs are wild enough to howl at the moon, but tame enough to stare right into our eyes and psychically declare, "Feed me." I have always tried to raise animals using Conscious Style principles. I never purchase harsh sprays, collars, and bedding from conventional stores; many of these products are saturated with irritating chemicals and end up hurting the animals. My rule: If I won't put it on my own skin, then it doesn't go on their fur. Instead I use common sense, purchase higher-quality ingredients, and invest the extra time in making homemade biscuits and shampoos.

Considering how seldom most animals complain and how much

unconditional love they offer us, I think taking a few extra steps to keep them healthy and happy is the least we can do. You can start by giving your pet the three basic things it needs in order to thrive: good nutrition, grooming, and warmth.

GOOD NUTRITION

Did you ever stop and wonder what you're feeding your cat or dog? The flesh of animals—cows, pigs, chickens—that fall into one of the four *D* categories (dead, dying, diseased, or disabled) is what ends up in most commercial pet foods. That kibble may contain cheap ingredients, such as ground-up feathers or deformed chicken legs unfit for human consumption. If you wouldn't eat it yourself, why feed it to your companion animals?

As I've stated earlier, I became a vegetarian when I was twelve years old. I made the switch to a meat-free diet after I learned about the cruelty and environmental degradation involved with factory farming. I've never been militant about it and have never forced my beliefs on other people. I simply did it out of my compassion for animals and the environment, and in the process created a healthy way of living that has accelerated my metabolism and given me lots of energy.

That's why I'm a big advocate of raising dogs on a vegetarian diet. Dogs are omnivores, just like us, and they do not need meat as part of their diet. A plethora of vegetarian dog food and supplements is available in most supermarkets today, and at competitive prices. You can order online and have veggie kibble sent directly to your home, too. These meat-free dog foods are nutritionally balanced—a high-quality alternative to regular brands.

Because dogs can be finicky eaters, buy several small bags of food; try out a few brands over the course of a week until you find the one Rover devours. This might also have you thinking, "Can I make my own homemade dog food?" Yes and no. While there are guides and books on making vegetarian dog food, I do not recommend it. There is an exact science to these recipes, and if you make the slightest error, your dog may receive inadequate protein, calcium, or vitamin D—all vitamins essential to their health.

Cats, on the other hand, are not omnivores, but carnivores. Veterinarians and companion animal experts have stated numerous times that it is not a good decision to raise a feline on a plant-based diet. And I agree. A vegetarian diet can cause loss of hearing, blindness, and problems with the heart. The best bet is to purchase high-quality canned food and mix it with a veterinarian-approved supplement. By avoiding processed "cat food" and spending a little bit more money on better-quality ingredients, you'll help your cat live a long and healthy life.

BONE APPETIT

I've never met a dog that didn't like this homemade treat. It's full of nutrition and flavor (and none of those artificial ingredients and ground-up who-knows-what), and even an old dog will learn new tricks for one of these.

    8 cups whole wheat flour
    1 cup nutritional yeast
    1½ tablespoons salt
    2 tablespoons garlic powder
    1 cup grated carrots
    3 cups water
    Barbecue sauce

Preheat oven to 400 degrees Fahrenheit. Mix the dry ingredients together. Add water 1 cup at a time until the mixture becomes a pliable dough. Roll out dough and cut with a dog-biscuit-shaped cookie cutter; place biscuits on parchment-lined cookie sheet. Brush barbecue sauce on each biscuit (top side only). Bake for 30 minutes, turn off the oven, and leave the biscuits in the oven overnight.

GROOMING

When I was a child, I raised a rottweiler–German shepherd puppy that I rescued from the street. I named her Ruebon after a dog I saw on a short-lived television sitcom. She was unusually strong and brave; I would often find her "playing" with a 15-foot

log or defending me from my shadow. The only thing she dreaded was being bathed. So when I had the rare opportunity to give her a bath, I thought I might as well do it right. To keep her clean and smelling sweet, I came up with this shampoo.

RUEBON'S SHAMPOO

Bunch of dried peppermint
(or 20 drops peppermint oil)
Bunch of dried spearmint
Bunch of dried sage
2 cups water
1 cup baby shampoo

Combine the herbs and water, and bring to boil. Turn off the heat and allow the "tea" to stand for 30 minutes. Strain the mixture, and combine the shampoo with the herbal water. Let shampoo cool and use immediately.

To prevent fleas, I also washed Ruebon in a citrus concoction. Take a small batch of oranges, grapefruit, lemons, and limes—all cut in half and juiced—and simmer the skins in a large pot of water for several hours. After the liquid cools, strain the water and pour a ¼ cup of the mixture over the dog's coat. It's not sticky, and the citrus oils greatly help in preventing fleas.

DEODORIZER

When she was just a year old, Ruebon got into a bit of a tussle with a skunk. The result: one foul-smelling pooch. A friend suggested the following recipe: After thoroughly washing the dog with regular shampoo (the kind you use), combine 1 quart of hydrogen peroxide, 1 cup each of baking soda and liquid soap; pour the mixture over the dog. Rinse man's best friend with warm water. It works!

WARMTH

He waits patiently all day long. Staring out the window . . . lying on the floor . . . staring out the window again. And then the door opens, and nothing matters more to him than the fact you're home!

Providing companionship and a warm place to sleep for your pets are thoughtful ways to give back to them. Yet, apart from a cardboard box full of old T-shirts and towels, many people hardly get the proper pet bedding at all.

A dog and cat need a place to call their own. To make beds a refuge for them, figure out where they like to sleep; then purchase a bed that best accommodates their preferences. If your cat likes sleeping on your soft duvet, bring a faux lamb's-wool bed into its sleeping area. If the dog likes being scratched behind the ears, consider a hemp bed stuffed with EcoSpun, a recycled plastic fleecelike material. The semi-rough fabric will feel nice against the dog's skin.

Exercise common sense: While silk covers, tassels, and a canopy may look pretty, they aren't really serving any purpose. Pets are rough-and-tumble animals; the delicate cover will fray, the tassels will get ripped, and the canopy—forget it, it's history after the first night. The best thing is to avoid froufrou bedding and look for beds that serve their purpose and do it simply and well. Comfort to a cat and dog is something soft and easy against the skin, not excessive ornamentation.

THE LAST WORD

Give one or two of these suggestions a try. Over time, I'm confident you'll make several of these ideas part of your regular cleaning regimen. You'll find that "green" solutions are also more effective and easier to use than conventional household products. And maybe you'll discover what I've known for years: Washing clothes with phosphate-free detergents does more than just clean them—it brings peace of mind.

WHERE I BOUGHT IT

All items featured in the book but not listed here are from private collections. All cooking utensils are from cooking.com, unless otherwise noted.

COVER: Danny Seo's shirt from Banana Republic, jeans from Gap.

INTRODUCTION: Danny Seo's pants from Banana Republic, jacket and T-shirt from Gap. Shot at the Antique Complex in Adamstown, PA.

CHAPTER ONE: LESS IS MORE: SORTING, STORING, AND MAINTAINING

Chalkboard paint from Cite Home, 100 Wooster St., New York, NY; (212) 431-7272. Metal locker bins from Cite Home. Recycling center from IKEA, www.ikea.com. Stainless-steel cart from Singer Equipment Company, 3030 Kutztown Rd., Reading, PA 19605; (610) 929-8000.

CHAPTER TWO: WALLS, WINDOWS, AND FLOORS

Café curtain rod from Kmart, www.bluelight.com. Café chair from Pottery Barn, www.potterybarn.com.

Custom bamboo blinds from AGIgroup.com, 1951 Porter Lake Dr., Suite E, Sarasota, FL 34240; (941) 377-5336; www.plantationshutter.com.

Bamboo flooring from EcoTimber, 1020 Heinz Ave., Berkeley, CA 94710; (888) 801-0855; www.ecotimber.com. Dried water hyacinth footstool from Smith & Hawken, www.smithandhawken.com.

LEFT: Browsing in one of my favorite stores in New York City, Lobels. **BELOW:** A tabletop grill made from recycled aluminum makes a great gift.

CHAPTER THREE: COOKING AND ENTERTAINING

Danny Seo's sweater by Donna Karan and pants by Banana Republic. Melissa Hick's sweater and jeans from Gap. Pillowcases from Pottery Barn. Recycled aluminum chair from Azcast Products, 15350 Proctor Ave., City of Industry, CA 91745; (626) 330-2177; www.azcastproducts.com. Coir rug from IKEA.

Chalkboard paint from Home Depot, www.homedepot.com.

Trophies from Fleetwood Antique Complex, RR 222, Fleetwood, PA 19522; (610) 944-0707. Recycled glass cups from GreenGlass. Hemp tablecloth from A Happy Planet (888) 946-4277; www.ahappyplanet.com.

CHAPTER FOUR: FURNITURE

Danny Seo's bandanna from Target, T-shirt and jeans from Gap. Citristrip is available at hardware stores nationwide or online at www.gaiam.com.

Galvanized vintage washtub from Adamstown Antique Mall. Recycled glass tumblers from IKEA. Galvanized tray from Restoration Hardware, www.restorationhardware.com. Towel rack from Anthropologie.

Church podium from Good Wood, 1428 U St. NW, Washington, DC 20009; (202) 986-3640. Blanket from Kmart.

CHAPTER FIVE: SANCTUARY

Organic cotton pillows from Terra Verde, 120 Wooster St., New York, NY 10012; (212) 925-4533; www.terraverde.com.

Plantation-grown hardwood armoire available at Oak Gallery, Route 10, Box 705, Morgantown, PA 19543; (610) 286-1718.

Mission table from Renningers Antique Mall and Flea Market, 2500 N Reading Rd., Denver, PA 17517; (717) 336-2177.

Lamp from Eddie Bauer Home, www.eddiebauer.com. Hand-forged butter knife from ABC Carpet and Home, 888 Broadway, New York, NY 10003; (212) 473-3000.

Slipcovers from Pottery Barn. Placemat from Anthropologie, www.anthropologie.com.

COLOR SECTION

Sofa covered in Polish hemp from Hemp Traders, www.hemptraders.com. Pillowcases from Banana Republic Home. Synthetic down pillow inserts from IKEA. Stained glass and Arts and Crafts–style chair from Adamstown Antique Mall. Unfinished wood plant stand from IKEA. Plantation-grown hardwood chest from Oak Gallery, Route 10, Box 705, Morgantown, PA 19543; (610) 286-1718. Sisal flooring from Hendricksen Naturlich Flooring, 7120 Keating Ave., Sebastopol, CA 95472; (707) 829-3959. Walls painted in HealthSpec Primitive Green paint from Sherwin-Williams. Sofa reupholstered by Radka's, 449 South 5th St., Reading, PA 19602; (610) 374-5701.

Natural grade maple floor from EcoTimber. Treetap from Zenway; www.zen-way.net. Two-hundred-year-old French ticking from Henro, 462 Broome St., New York, NY 10013; (212) 343-0221.

Bamboo flooring from EcoTimber. Organic cotton bedding from Coyuchi, 11101 State Route 1, Point Reyes Station, CA 94956; (888) 418-8847; www.coyuchi.com. Lighting and synthetic down duvet from IKEA. Organic buckwheat hull pillow from Terra Verde. Phone from Office Depot, www.of-ficedepot.com.

Kitchen cabinets from IKEA. Stainless-steel table and stainless-steel storage bin from Singer Equipment Supply. Range hood from Sears, www.sears.com. Natural grade maple floor from EcoTimber. Japanese stainless-steel food container from Urban Outfitters, www.urbn.com. Vintage clock from Adamstown Antique Mall. Frames from IKEA. Kitchen installed by Don McCullough Construction, 783 White Oak Ln., Leesport, PA 19533; (610) 926-3790. Flooring installed by Berks Flooring Specialties, 215 S 5th Ave., Reading, PA 19611; (610) 378-7828.

Hemp tablecloth from A Happy Planet. Bandanna napkins from Target. Dining room chairs reupholstered by Radka's in hemp from Hemp Traders. Walls painted with HealthSpec paint from Sherwin-Williams. Oyster candles from Smith & Hawken.

Recycled glass tile from Sandhill Industries, 1896 Marika Rd., Fairbanks, AL 99709; (907) 451-6508.

Sink from Waterworks, 469 Broome St., New York, NY 10013; (212) 966-0605; www.waterworks.com. Star lighting fixture from Mosaic House Moroccan Imports, 62 W. 22nd St., New York, NY 10010; (212) 414-2525. Plant stand from IKEA. Squeeze bottle from Singer Equipment Supply. Ceiling painted with HealthSpec paint from Sherwin-Williams. Walls painted with recycled latex paint from Amazon Environmental, P.O. Box 9306, Whittier, CA 90608.

Recycled aluminum chairs from Azcast Products (626) 330-2177. Fish statue from Adamstown Antique Mall, 94 N Lancaster Ave., Adamstown, PA 19501; (717) 484-0464. Coir rug from IKEA. Matchstick blinds from IKEA. Wicker furniture from Lloyd Flanders, www.lloydflanders.com. Deck painted with Behr Premium Plus Paint, www.behrpaint.com.

Recycled glass bowl from Fire and Light, P.O. Box 95518, Arcata, CA 95518; (800) 944-2223. Polished river rock from Smith & Hawken. Plates from Reading China and Glass, Reading, PA. Hemp tablecloth from Gaiam. Buntal pillow from Banana Republic Home, www.bananarepublic.com. Recycled metal star from Black Angus Antique Mall, Route 272, Adamstown, PA 19501; (717) 484-4386. Lights from Smith & Hawken. Metal numbers from Anthropologie.

Recycled aluminum hoseguards from Azcast Products. Danny Seo's clothing by Gap. Recycled rubber hose from Home Depot.

Plants from garden.com. Bamboo stakes from Kmart. Willow edging from Smith & Hawken.

CHAPTER SIX: REFRESH

Recycled aluminum bathroom fixtures from Azcast Products. Biodegradable toothbrush from Waterworks. Organic cotton towels from Coyuchi.

CHAPTER SEVEN: WORKING @ HOME

Plantation-grown hardwood chair from Oak Gallery. Recycled aluminum desktop accessories from Gaiam. Recycled aluminum file holder from Restoration Hardware. Recycled paper pencils from Wal-Mart, www.wal-mart.com. Hand-hammered copper trash can from Smith & Hawken. Vintage wood desk from Black Angus Antique Mall.

Hemp duvet cover from Calvin Klein Home. Synthetic down duvet from Eddie Bauer Home. Filing cabinet from Staples, www.staples.com. Citristrip available at hardware stores nationwide. Striped pillow from Banana Republic Home.

CHAPTER EIGHT: DECORATIVE ACCESSORIES

Camera Club prints from Fleetwood Antique Complex. Wall painted with HealthSpec paint from Sherwin-Williams.

Vintage globe from Fleetwood Antique Complex.

CHAPTER NINE: OUTDOORS

Candles from Pier 1 Imports, www.pier1.com. Chairs and table from Fleetwood Antique Complex. Hanging lanterns from Pottery Barn. Recycled glass tableware from Fire and Light, P.O. Box 95518, Arcata, CA 95518; (800) 944-2223. Recycled aluminum grill from Azcast Products. Hemp napkins from Gaiam, www.gaiam.com.

All garden edging from Smith & Hawken.

CHAPTER TEN: TAKING CARE

Energy-efficient bulbs from IKEA and Home Depot.

Eco-friendly cleaners available at Gaiam.com.

INDEX